Counterpoints

Believing christian faith in a difficult world

Vernon White

Published by Sarum College Press.

ISBN 0 9534836 6 5

Sarum College Press
19 The Close, Salisbury
Wiltshire SP1 2EE
01722 326899
bookshop@sarum.ac.uk
www.sarumcollegebookshop.co.uk

The author and publisher gratefully acknowledge permission to reprint extracts from Collected Poems by Edwin Muir published by Faber and Faber Ltd.

For Patrick

I was a stranger, could not read these people
Or this outlandish deity. Did a God
Indeed in dying cross my life that day
By chance, he on his road and I on mine?

And now that time grows shorter, I perceive
That Plato's is the truest poetry,
And that these shadows
Are cast by the true

Edwin Muir

Preface

Counterpoints is a series of 'soundbites' on central areas of christian belief. It is an attempt to provide short reflections on key issues of faith in a way which renews confidence in mainstream christian believing, while facing the difficulties squarely. It is, at heart, a proclamation of faith and belief - but always in relation to the searching or sceptical question.

Although its origin lies in teaching and preaching carried out over many years and in a variety of contexts, it has been developed, edited and organized into a genre of its own (it is not a book of sermons or talks). Its style is idiosyncratic. It is sometimes personal, occasionally homiletic, but also relates to a good deal of underlying academic discussion. It addresses complex debates with compressed references, aiming to be brisk and uncluttered but without over-simplifying. There are no footnotes or academic apparatus.

It should appeal to thoughtful people of faith, half-faith, or lapsed faith - especially those who have no time to read long chapters in dense books, but who are hungry for hard thought in digestible chunks. Students, ministers, ordinands, lay church study groups, theologians, teachers, are amongst those who might find it most helpful. But it is important to be clear what it seeks to be helpful about. It is not a book about Church life and order. It is simply about trying to believe in God, and trying to live honestly in the light of that belief.

Contents

Introduction

This book is a sequence of short essays on the credibility of christian belief in a world where belief is hard to sustain. It arises from trying to teach and preach the christian faith, but also from trying to *believe* it. The two, I find, are inseparable. I cannot begin to teach what I have not faced as an issue of belief. At the same time I cannot continue to believe anything without in some way trying to teach it, or give expression to it - or live it.

In this double-sided process a pattern emerges. All teaching and believing involve a kind of counterpoint between the questions of experience and the response of faith. The questions take shape inexorably in a world where faith is difficult: they are existential and intellectual in form, questions of heart, soul and mind. The response of faith engages with them in similar form: faith also involves heart, soul and mind.

This correlation (Paul Tillich's term) between the questions existence throws up and the view that faith provides is complex. In favoured moments our existence seems to present secure stepping stones to faith. We pass from one to the other without stumbling. Occasionally, existence simply *is* faith. There seems no journey to travel at all. At other times they barely meet at all, except as outright antagonists. Dancing partners at one moment, sparring partners the next. Counterpoint, then: a metaphor of harmony and contradiction.

Put another way, I realize there has always been a trace of apologetics in the way I teach and believe. I do not mean apologetics as rational persuasion, but in a looser sense of 'making connections'. Perhaps this is true of all christian teaching and believing, in some degree. To acknowledge the abiding difficulty of faith, and to want to address it by looking for points of connection with wider thought and experience, is intrinsic to almost any sort of faith. Modernity and post-modernity makes the difficulty of faith inevitable: the present world's sceptical and plural nature provides a testing backdrop to any belief. So too does the rapidity of change. The pace of change moves us so swiftly to the next horizon of meaning that it becomes harder than ever to take *any* view with conviction. The counterpoint of apologetic then becomes the inevitable response. It is the task of spotting both the connections and contradictions between faith and experience. It means exploring and exposing the nature of both. It makes no pretence to provide proofs of God's existence, but it does show the connections to be real and vital.

What doctrinal suppositions lie behind this sort of teaching and believing?

Some sort of natural theology is at work: there is the supposition of a general revelation to make the connections possible. But the heart of it also presupposes, and expounds, a specific revelation. It is a faith which is shaped by specific revelatory events and experiences, generating their own language and concepts. This means there are 'regulative' principles at work (a term used by George Lindbeck). Amongst these are the reality of one Trinitarian God; the frailty and fallibility (fallenness) of the human condition; the partial, progressive, revelation of that God within the history of Israel; God's pivotal revelation in Jesus Christ. All these exert their pressure on what is being said in this book, and I express them with some confidence.

Is such confidence at odds with the counterpoint of questions, the backdrop of plurality, difficulty, and doubt? Not necessarily. Some kind of confidence is intrinsic to all proclamation, a proper form of all christian teaching and preaching. Confidence is also the way we test our believing. So I am content to leave a positive note of proclamation sounding within this book. There is something of dogma here, as well as something of socratic dialogue. I make no bones about it because it is the combination of hard questions and confident proclamation that helps true belief.

This does not mean the book is simply a record of 'kerygma', like a book of talks or sermons. There are some elements of normal homiletic proclamation, such as detailed Biblical exposition, which do not feature. Other elements of argument, reflection, and imagination feature rather more. This is to help draw out the pattern of counterpoint and apologetic more clearly. The material has further been arranged broadly in the order of systematic theology (Revelation, God, Christ, Salvation, Holy Spirit, Ethics) and, more loosely, according to the church calendar (Christmas, Easter, Pentecost). It ends with a very simple short story - a parable which reminds me, and the reader, that *any* attempt to portray God is perilous.

But it is still necessary to try. Although circumstance and temperament have forced many of us to live uneasily between faith and experience, we have to articulate faith in some way. It is too important to stay silent. If these short reflections help even in the smallest degree to sustain a more confident christian faith with integrity in such a difficult world, I shall be more than satisfied.

* The personal pronoun 'He' is used throughout for God, to retain a sense of the personal nature of God: but it should not be taken to mean that God is exclusively male.

1. Truth, Fantasy, Revelation

A first set of questions for faith to face has to do with our propensity to make things up. We suspect we may be inventing truth, not discovering it. Especially in matters of religion. This realization is not new - we have always been inclined to create God, to satisfy our own vested interests. The disciplines of social anthropology and psychology have now made us much more aware of how and why we might be doing it.

This fact of our inventiveness is indisputable. But pondering it has led me to ask some counter questions as well. If we have made things up about God (and ourselves) *what has led us to do so? With what resources have we 'made things up'? Where have the ideas of our inventions come from?*

In the rest of life a moment's reflection makes us realize that most of our inventions derive from a mixture of what is already within us *and* what really exists beyond us. Where else do the characters of our fiction come from but the interaction of our imagination with real people whom we have encountered as *others,* people existing beyond us as well as within us? The imagination within has been fed, at some stage, from something or someone real beyond us. In other words, when we create we do not create *ex nihilo.* In one way or another we create out of something real which is (or was) beyond, something which has encountered us and helped create the resources out of which we ourselves 'invent'.

So when we come to religious ideas here too we should moderate some of our suspicions about invention. The distinction between 'truth' and 'invention' in religion, as in other things, may not be so easily drawn after all. Much religion may well be constructed, but some of the building blocks may also carry a truth from beyond, a transcendent truth. At the very least we should keep an open mind about it.

But how do we make the distinction within the mix? What (and where) is the truly transcendent truth within it all? How do we know when and where we are just seeing a mirror of self-interest, and where we are seeing a reflection from something really beyond ourselves?

This question, I find, cannot be answered only by general principles or generalities of experience. It needs also to be answered in a *particular* way. Such as the way and truth and life of Jesus Christ. That is an answer which will not necessarily satisfy just in cold print. The truth of Jesus Christ has to be lived and experienced in order to be believed. That is a consequence of realizing that truth is not just a commodity we can pluck from general experience, nor just from abstract argument and speculative thought. It will emerge just as much, and more, from engaging actively with particular people and situations (a point well made by liberation theologians). Only this way will the questions of truth, fantasy, and revelation ultimately be settled.

Such are some of the issues of this first section, which begins speculatively, but ends very firmly rooted in the particular and concrete reality of Jesus Christ.

1.1. Cloud-Cuckoo Land: Fantasy, Reality, God

Fantasy is a common human pastime, and an all-age one. We begin with Peter Pan, then pass through science fiction, computer games, and (tragically) drugs. Throughout adulthood we still fantasize, constructing improbable futures for ourselves, mixing desire and curiosity in our imaginative journeys of the mind.

It is an ancient pastime, as well as a modern one. The legendary dreams of past peoples seeth with strange sea-monsters, beheaded warriors who come back to life, and so on. 'Cloud-cuckoo land' itself dates back to Aristophanes' comedy *The Birds* (414 B.C.). Two Athenians are dissatisfied with their life and decide to build a new city in the sky called Nephelokokkygia: cloud-cuckoo land. This illuminates enduring ingredients of human nature: it is not only desire and curiosity but also dissatisfaction, boredom, restlessness, escapism, which motivate our imagination and drive our dreams.

So much for the origins of fantasy. But what of its substance? Whence and why the *oddity* which characterizes it? Why such weird and grotesque creatures, such extraordinary and unlikely events? This may prove even more interesting to unravel because it begs an important question: how do we measure oddness and improbability anyway?

The answer, I suspect, is the answer of Ecclesiastes. Just as there is nothing new under the sun, so there is nothing truly odd. The furniture of our fantasies is really made out of familiar things from the real world, twisted into different combinations, transposed into different contexts, enhanced with unusual powers - but still fundamentally recognizable. Consider the characters and events of *Lord of the Rings, Star Trek, Harry Potter, Star Wars* or your own private dreams, and you will see the point. Fantasy and reality are not wholly different things: they are made out of each other, intersect each other, depend on each other.

The same point is reversible. How can we be sure that 'ordinary' reality is not itself an oddity or an improbability? Take trees as an example. Conduct a simple thought experiment. Step back from them and forget their familiarity. They are extraordinary: they are great tangled monsters of convoluted arms which roar and shake in the wind, reaching prodigious heights, changing colour and shedding their clothes to reveal grotesque skeletons beneath. Or what about the wind itself? It is an insinuous, ghostly thing, blowing invisibly where it will. What about the oceans - and the outlandish life within them? And what about humanity - ourselves? Suspend familiarity with ourselves and we may suddenly realize that we too are '*fearfully and wonderfully made*' (Psalm 139). Consider human history and personal narrative and we will find staggering true stories of men and women reaching heights of nobility, depths of viciousness, extraordinary achievements of mind, body and spirit - which may seem utterly improbable. In the end, even the very fact of anything *being* is a matter of awe: I am dumbfounded by the stone or the sage equally, for they exist.

Thus truth and fiction alike are strange, or alike familiar: they are not as much as odds with each other as they sometimes seem. Yes, some forms of retreat into fantasy are dangerous or absurd, but that cannot be the whole truth about it. We should beware of being too supercilious about our fantasies because our dreams may be more real than we think. We should beware of being too superficial about our reality because there is more to that than we think.

To think again about God, eternity, a world beyond this world, must therefore be to think in the same way. Its oddness may only be *prima facie.* Its 'fantastic' quality may need a more careful response. Think again about the strange story of the God who entered this world to live and die and rise again. Is it really so strange? Or does this, too, trail some half-recognized sense of familiarity with it? *Just* cloud-cuckoo land? Beware the 'just'! If so-called reality and so-called fantasy intertwine so much, we might think again before dismissing it all as mere fantasy. If the real world itself can seem so improbable (yet exists), why not God as well?

1.2. Aches and Fears: the Mother of Invention, the Route of Revelation

A crack of thunder, a nightmare, or just some unaccountable frisson of fear - and a young child runs to its mother. The mother, instinctively, gathers the child up: *'It's all right'*, she says, *'everything is all right'*.

And so, some say, religion is born: religion is constructed. It is born precisely out of that deep need for reassurance we all have in a hostile world. It is a reassurance we temporarily find (if we are lucky) in our earthly parents. But we need more. So we project our parents into the heavens. We come to believe in a divine Father figure. Our ache for security is so great we invent God - and then hand Him down in religious beliefs and practices over the centuries. Such religion makes us feel safe - it can also be moulded to bolster our sense of purpose and value, our personal (or national) pride and identity.

The trouble comes when we *realize* it may all have been invented, just a projection of needs and desires. That is the unnerving revelation of Freud, Feuerbach, Durkheim.

For some the realization is liberating. If we have been brought up in an oppressive religion then the possibility that it was all invented helps free us. If we encounter a religion of national or ethnic identity which ferments fanaticism the possibility that this is just a human perversion helps us resist it. What is only invented is all the more easily discarded or criticised. For others it is disturbing. We feel the frisson of fear more deeply still. If there really are no everlasting arms beneath the mother's arms, then this is terrifying indeed. It means everything is not 'all right' - *not even in the end.*

The idea that religion may be invented is not entirely new. It is not just an insight of modern psychology or anthropology of which ancient cultures were naively unaware. We have long been aware that religion can be a human construct. The Hebrews' complaint against idols of other religions is an early example: *'they have mouths but they do not speak; eyes, but do not see; they have ears, but do not hear...'* (Psalm 115) . In other words, they are made up.

It is also the basis of a complaint against their own religion whenever the 'true' God who claims to have made Himself known is reconstructed to suit the people's own purposes. This was the burden of Jeremiah's prophecy to the insecure and politically vulnerable people of the 7th century B.C. These people of Israel knew their real security was in a covenant - a moral and personal relationship with God and each other, given and renewed at key moments in their history of Noah, Abraham, Moses and the ten commandments. They knew their true safety and proper pride lay in keeping that covenant, and in returning to it when they failed. But they had not done this. Their trust had shifted from relationship with the living God Himself to the outward and visible sign of Him: the Temple and its worship. They had reconstructed their God as the God of the Temple, rather than the God of covenant relationship. They refashioned God as a symbol of what they wanted the Temple to represent: national superiority and security - rather than the God who dwelt in the Temple only by grace and only within the terms of the covenant relationship. So Jeremiah weighed in, mimicking, mocking, scathing: *'You come and stand before me in this house, which is called by my name, and say "we are safe!" ... .. this is the Temple of the Lord, the Temple of the Lord .... But do not trust in these deceptive words.... Amend your ways and your doings ....'* (Jeremiah 7)

Seven centuries later the Jesus of John's Gospel reminded a woman of something similar. She is told to beware confining God to worship in Jerusalem, on this mountain or anywhere else, to beware taking refuge in particular places or observable religious practices. Instead, she is told that *'God is spirit and those who worship him must worship in spirit and truth'* (John 4). She is confronted with a truth that is to be found instead in Christ Himself, the great *I am* who transcends (and judges) all religions.

This does not mean we can dispense with all observable, communal, religious practices. Of course we cannot. If there is a God at all He will surely meet us through them. But the risk of them is always present. They are too easily made into a false refuge, self-justifying, an evasion of the very God they are supposed to mediate. *'In religion man can bolt and bar himself against God'*, said Karl Barth, a twentieth century prophet, echoing Jeremiah.

But although religion has always been constructed, note this: in the past this did not usually mean complete reductionism. It did not mean that the actual reality of God Himself was thought to be created. Not for one moment did past prophets think that *all* sense of God was invention. False gods there were, but the real God still pressed upon them through the prophets. He was still believed to be there - to deconstruct the false constructions, to expose the shallow short-cuts to safety, to offer a deeper security.

Should it be any different now? Have the insights of psychology and anthropology added something fundamentally new? I do not think so. They have made us more aware of the *mechanisms* by which we create (and often distort) meaning for ourselves - but that is all. Analysis of such mechanisms does not answer the question of ultimate truth and meaning.

After all, in general experience we do not normally reckon that to uncover the mechanisms of our needs and desires is to find nothing but signs of illusion, invention, distortion. If anything it is the opposite: our needs and desires are more usually taken as signs that there is something beyond, a prior reality which stimulates those very needs and desires (which can then distort it). Take some of the simplest signs: our craving for possessions does not mean there is nothing real to possess, even though it helps explain how we make idols of them; our need for esteem and friendship does not mean there are no real people or relationships to enjoy, even though it may help generate false images of those other people. So why should it be any different with our ache for security and for God? This too may be a sign of a real God, even though it also leads us to invention and distortion about Him. Real things, people and God alike come before us and transcend us even as we distort them through the powerful and complex instincts of our desires. We have not wholly invented things just because we ache for them.

All this means our basic instincts are bound to be double-edged. Our need for security is clearly like this. Yes, it easily seduces us to invent a god and evade the real God. Equally, it is a sign of a real God who will also be a real security to us. So the instinct is a pathway for two-way traffic. It carries our own perilous constructions: but it also conveys an ultimate truth. It is a route for our religion: but it is also a route for God's real revelation.

Something similar could be said of fear, particularly the fear of God. It is a dangerous doctrinal tool in the hands of parents or politicians who wish to repress and oppress. That part is the invention. But fear is also a proper sign of God's reality. We fear things, people, and God precisely because of their transcendent reality, because they have a being of their own which can resist us. Even a stone can trip us up. The otherness of a person with their own resistant will is an even greater force to be reckoned with, in any real relationship. Even more so with God, if He is real. In this way fear can be a proper reflection of God's reality, a reassurance that we are *not* just making up our cosy projections of Him.

This point can be pressed. Too comfortable a picture of God is ultimately unbelievable - we are almost bound to have made Him up. But a less comfortable God who meets us in resistance as well as acceptance, who loves us (when necessary) like a surgeon - He commands more credibility. We may run away at first from this bracing full measure of reality. It is natural to run scared from the Hound of Heaven. *But at least we know it is real.* And so in the end we are more likely to run full circle, back into His arms. Children and parents alike, we all need refuge - but it must be a true one.

Thus the counterpoint of projection and reflection runs through all our deepest instincts. They are both there. That is the pivotal point within it all. There is a reflection from beyond as well as a projection onto it. There is revelation. We have not made it all up.

1.3. What (and Where) is Truth?

If there is a God then truth is something to do with God - obviously. But how does that help? What (and where) is God? Is not God everywhere - and therefore nowhere in particular? So how could we discern Him and His ways? Must God not be beyond all knowing? *'As the heavens are higher than the earth, so are my ways higher than your ways, and my thoughts are higher than your thoughts'* says the Lord of Isaiah 55.

Liberalism responds by spreading the search as widely as possible. It looks through the whole history of religion and religious experience, through secular history and experience, seeking the sum of all God's thoughts and ways in the totality of things. A mosaic is fashioned out of insights from every science and every religion, comprehensive, open-ended.

This is a rational response, dating from the days when rationality was celebrated with great confidence. Is not reason the common thread of divine disclosure throughout the whole of creation? This means that the divine hand should not be excluded from any part of the creation - and our reason should be reliable enough to discern it.

It is also an instinctive response. It seems generous and democratic. Even if reason is no longer trusted so much, we still naturally feel that truth must be universally available, widely scattered, unrestricted. We assume it will be all the *truer* for being *bigger.* The instincts and intentions of casting the net wide are honourable.

But for all that it might still be misconceived. When we search for truth about meaning and value we are in a particular kind of landscape where the broad view is not necessarily the best. Truth about meaning and value is not gleaned simply from an amalgam of knowledge and a breadth of experience (though such breadth may also help). A television producer, engineer, and a compulsive viewer, might all pool their knowledge to judge the true meaning and worth of a programme. But that of itself would not guarantee a better judgement than a single astute viewer might provide. That is because this sort of truth is not just a general commodity gathered up *quantitively* in our life-experience. As story-tellers know, it is also a specific *quality* of experience. It is a particular way of seeing things, rather than a collection of many things.

This means that the particular may mediate the truth better than the universal. Women and men of wide experience do not necessarily have all the answers. They may need the wisdom of the humble hermit or the clear sight of a child. As Ivan Karamazov needs Alyosha; as Shakespearian Kings need their fool. It also means that truth may be mediated through particular deeds, rather than general ideas. As the power and glory of Graham Greene's great novel is constituted in a single defining act of sacrifice from a poor whiskey priest, or as the pivot of many a plot lies in one moment in a soliloquy, or one fatal act.

This emerges in real life, not just fiction. As the American theologian Reinhold Niebuhr has pointed out, the collective morality of a state is inferior to its individual parts. It tends to a lowest common denominator, inferior to the morality of the average individual citizen. So it is always preferable for the morality of the state to be directed by the example of individual citizens rather than the morality of individual citizens to be directed by the state. It is the same point. Moral truth, like all truth of meaning and value, is a specific quality best revealed and grasped in particular words and deeds: better expressed in the individual person than in the generality of things.

Why is this? Why is truth better grasped and conveyed in the particular? Perhaps because truth has to do with seeing distinctions and relations between things (morally, spiritually, empirically, factually). And we can only make those distinctions between things if we have truly understood any one thing. So we must concentrate on particular things, as well as look more widely. Range widely and superficially and we will see little. Go deep into one small world and we may see better when we look everywhere else as well. It is the Miss Marple principle of detection: by entering deeply and fully into the life of her small village, she gains the wisdom to solve crimes from a much wider world. It is a view of truth which is neither classically modern (too wary of particulars) nor radically post-modern (too imprisoned within particulars). But it is a common sense view.

It is also the principle of orthodox Christian faith. It is why there is a scandal of particularity at the heart of faith. God reveals Himself in the particularity of Jesus Christ. That is why the Christian task is not the same as the liberal task. It is not first of all the task of collating God's ways and thoughts as they are scattered generally throughout the world: it is the very particular task of coming to terms with Jesus Christ. This helps explain one of the greatest moments of dramatic irony in history: the moment when Pilate asks (with Jesus standing in front of him) *'what is truth?'*. It was a general, abstract, and evasive question: since he knew he could not face a particular answer he asked a general question. But the answer was particular. It stood before him in flesh and blood

So it is not surprising that we are often advised that we must hold fast to particularity in Christian faith. And this means we are bound to encounter what seems to be an illiberal tone. Like this from the writer to Timothy: *'For the time is coming when people will not put up with sound doctrine but, having itching ears, they will accumulate for themselves teachers to suit their own desires... But you, hold to the standard of sound teaching that you have learned from me, in the faith and love that are in Christ Jesus'* (2 Timothy 1,4). No doubt this is a warning strongly coloured by the human insecurities of early Church leaders: it may well have to do with the frightened dogmatism of vested interests; we may be listening to leaders wanting power and needing their congregations to toe the line. But for all that, does it not also reflect this deeper truth about truth? Is it not also the simple reminder that ultimate truths may be found through a particular person and in one particular story?

Tolerantly and persuasively we shall often be asked this question: why insist that the particularity of Christ is so special? Why not simply set him alongside many other things, as just one source of truth amongst others? Why not acknowledge a relativism or pluralism of religious truth which makes all differences equal and nothing in particular with special authority? We probably ask the same question of ourselves. We ask the question all the more urgently in the current climate of religious conflict. But we still have this answer to reckon with. Particularity is the way truths are shaped when they are about ultimate value and true meaning. So we cannot ignore the power in particular truth, the cutting edge in Christ. It is the way they first believed: perhaps it is the only way we can continue to believe.

This does not mean we should make truth more scandalous than it need be. Truth (and God) is also everywhere else, and must be sought everywhere else. In the terms of John's Gospel (Ch.1) *'the 'word made flesh'* is also *'the light which enlightens everyone'.* For the point is not that truth is excluded from the generality of things, only that it cannot be constituted and grasped *just* by generality. This means that there is plenty of liberality in the end. Once we have submitted to the discipline of the particular, then the whole world is ours to explore after all. Seen through the lens of Jesus Christ, the whole world is the Lord's and all that is in it. Conservative, blinkered, hidebound, dangerously exclusive? Not at all. Once we have been properly pinned down by the particular, then we are released to be more liberal and inclusive than ever. We must go back to every nook and cranny of the universe, to every highway and by-way of knowledge, every religious and secular pathway of knowledge. There will indeed be something of God there and everywhere.

Nonetheless, this belief remains - we shall only truly see God everywhere if we look for Him, live Him, and experience Him, in something particular. And a Christian can do no other than testify that this happens especially in Jesus Christ.

2. Creation, History, Providence

Another set of questions for faith to address has to do with our place in the universe. We only have to consider it seriously for a moment to feel insecure. A more sustained reflection on it is likely to make us even more bewildered. It makes us realize we are the hapless victims of an unsettling paradox.

The problem is this. On the one hand we have been trained to have an ever greater sense of self-awareness. This is part of our Enlightenment inheritance. Since Descartes' dictum (*'I think therefore I am'*) we have tried to find our identity in our own reasoning, thinking, choosing. It makes us acutely self-aware. But on the other hand the Enlightenment legacy has also eroded the setting in which this intense 'centred' self belongs. Under the scrutiny of scientific reason the surrounding universe has become larger and more inhospitable, a context of chance rather than a home by design. Human culture, tradition, and faith communities have become equally insecure, withered by scepticism, weakened by relativism - and we are detached from what remains of them by that same lure of individual thought and choice which we were taught to prize so much.

This leaves the individual self in a disorientating dilemma. We have been led to believe we matter more and more - but we are less and less secure in our sense of belonging anywhere. It is hard to sustain a sense of personal meaning and significance in such a situation. It is a form of suffering. It poses hard questions to faith.

How does faith deal with this? I suggest it produces its own paradox in response.

On the one hand, when the universe makes us feel small,

accidental, overwhelmed, faith points uncompromisingly to the greatness of God. *God* is not overwhelmed by the hugeness of the universe. The creator's possibilities, by definition, must outrank the mystery and massiveness of the creation. And because of this transcendence God can still care for the detail - you and me - within the whole. In this way faith reassures us. On the other hand, when self-consciousness is inflating our self-importance, faith takes us to task. That same transcendence of God means we should not presume to know or ask too much. In the face of Almighty God, too much clamour for attention from our selves sounds suspiciously like arrogance or egoism.

God therefore becomes both the reason for reassurance and for judgement. Faith and forgiveness will both be needed when we seriously consider our place in the universe. That is the real burden of this next set of reflections on creation, history, providence.

2.1 Feeling Small, Believing Big

In the beginning, perhaps twelve billion years ago, the world sprang forth. It began (probably) from what is called the big bang. In the tiniest fraction of a second space boiled out in rapid expansion. For a moment it was all just hot. But as it cooled, matter and radiation emerged. Gravity began to balance the outward explosion in a more stable order. Within that fine-tuned balance lumps of matter, galaxies, stars, began to form. After five billion years these first stars began to die, and their dying dust became (probably) the stuff of life on earth. That life evolved. Wondrously, through a complex and (surely) guided process, jellyfish and worms left the seas, dinosaurs appeared and disappeared. Eventually *homo sapiens* got to his and her feet and walked the planet. Mind, consciousness, spirit, prayer, dawned. The universe had become aware of itself - and of its Maker.

Then the first movements of human organization and civilisation became visible. They too swelled, as if in another big bang, exploding into the myriad cultures of our world history. They stretched through time and space to include all manner of human living and being: Kalahari bushmen, instinctive mystics of nature; towering heights of Ancient Greek and Roman culture; Arabic philosophy; Chinese and Buddhist dynasties; great semitic religions; Christendom; the western history of Enlightenment and scientific achievement. This accumulated knowledge and experience has become prodigious. Not only has the universe become aware of itself, it has become more aware than ever of its own immensity.

We have also become more aware of its end. For this fine-tuned balance is not likely to hold for ever. The universe will (probably) implode, or disintegrate. A heat-death, perhaps. And shall not we disappear with it? From star dust we were made, and to dust we shall return.

So I wonder. As I look at the night sky, or at the multitudes of people crowding past me on a pavement, I wonder both at the vastness of things and at their transience. And I wonder, therefore, about our significance as individuals. I wonder what God's plan and purpose could possible be. Does God really care what we are when each of us is such a tiny, transient, player on such a huge stage? Does He even care for cultures or civilizations as a whole, or the universe as a whole?

Such wonder prompts a kind of dizziness, a metaphysical vertigo, sometimes a gnawing fear. But it might also provoke faith, even hope. It all depends.

For a start we might reflect more on the significance of size. Rightly we wonder at the immensity of time and space. But is quantity the only thing to wonder at? Not at all. Take a piece of music. It is not valuable or significant just because it is long. Better still, consider a person. A person is not better or more valuable because she has lived longer - or because he is taller. Neither music nor people are measured in that way. Their significance is not measured in time and space. The loveliness of music or the beauty of holiness in a person can be expressed in the tiniest tract of time or space and be not a whit less lovely or holy for that. The fact that each individual human person is but a speck of dust in a huge and crowded universe is immaterial. It does not diminish their significance and value one iota.

The significance of size could even be turned on its head. The vastness of the universe might be a tribute to human significance, not an affront. If it took the labour of twelve billion years, the birth and death of countless stars, to fashion us, perhaps that tells us how much we are worth. We are worth *all that* effort.

This does not mean the universe is only a process to produce us, a stage for us to strut on. The Lord of the universe delights in it for its own sake, as well as for ours. If we forget that then we shall indeed be cut down to size. As God acidly asked Job: *'Where were you when I laid the foundation of the earth ..? Who laid its cornerstone when the morning stars sang together?'* (Job 38). We were nowhere. But the stars were there. They were rejoicing their creator, singing God's praises. Just as everything else that is made rejoices God: the hills which *'gird themselves with joy'*, the valleys which *'deck themselves with grain, they shout and sing together for joy'*, (Psalm 65), the lilies of the field which are *'clothed in glory'* (Matthew 6).

In the same way, cultures and civilizations are not just settings for individuals. They matter in themselves and can rejoice the creator. That is why God formed a *people* for Himself, a social enterprise: the people of Israel, and the new Israel of the Church. That is why St. Paul tells us to respect and value social and political orders.

In short - the immensity of things does not diminish the individual, but nor does the significance of individuals diminish the rest of creation. We are not to be dewy-eyed environmentalists so rapt with the world that we cease to value human persons. But nor are we to be arrogant human individualists who belittle that wider world. God values us as individuals and as a whole. The glory is in both - and in the interrelation between both.

Nonetheless, this other angst remains. Perhaps we matter while we live - but are we not still transient? Does not some heat-death or other destruction doom us (and all creation) to nothing? What is more, would we want creation or humanity to survive, even if we could? We are so flawed. The creation may be wondrous, but it also groans with travail. Its peoples and cultures are fashioned out of pain and conflict, forged from a freedom which has permitted rampant evil. Wonder has to be clear-eyed about all this. Doubt, dizziness, fear, return all too easily.

But again, it all depends. Faith and hope are still possible. To begin with the flaws: of course they are there, but they are not all that is there. Creation may be groaning with discord, but good tunes have also been played. The tortuous paths of natural history have still produced the loveliness of stars and sunshine, hills and valleys, brave spring flowers. The tortured paths of human history have still produced courage and compassion and moments of justice. Cultural history has still achieved its great art and architecture. The universe may be a flawed, cumbersome, and transient instrument, but all this fine music has still been played on it. Such music is scattered, momentary, sometimes barely more than a single short melody, but it has still been composed and played uniquely within this strange universe. At one point God has even performed it to perfection: in Jesus Christ. A small moment in the vastness of space and time - but remember, not a whit less significant for that. In fact, that note of perfection was so significant it even sounds in eternity. It was simply too good to lose. Christ died as we shall all die - *but He was also raised.*

This turns our attention to transience as well. Will that really have the final word? Or might other good things be raised as well, perfected in a Christ-like image?

Somehow, through Christ, they can and will. The promise is there, the sign has been given.

This is the meaning of the resurrection of the body: all the good that is fashioned through this physical universe will not be wasted; it will be taken up to eternity, *'an inheritance that is imperishable, undefiled, and unfading, kept in heaven'* (I Peter 1). What has been created through this flawed and fading physical instrument can and will be replayed on a new instrument: a new heaven and earth. It means that we may 'replay' both the spiritual and sensual good of this universe. We shall not just be spirits beginning some new and unrelated existence in heaven, as if this universe had never been. We shall be able to re-inhabit all the good that came out of it. Perhaps, in some strange way, I shall be able to take you through an English meadow in spring, the bushman will be able to show me the sunrise over the Kalahari, and we shall taste again the love and laughter of all our lives.

This, is one of the best of all counterpoints: transient we may be, but transience itself will come to an end. That is the hope which the most significant small point in all this twelve billion years holds out - for us all.

2.2 Is it all *Meant*? On the Possibility of Providence

In childhood I thought everything was happening for me. My picture of God's activity was almost entirely self-centred. When things went wrong it was a warning for me. When things went right it was an encouragement for me. It was all *meant.* Every event, and especially coincidences, seemed momentous with divine meaning. I played games with patterns of events. It adds an edge of excitement, to see what each day will bring, if you believe that it is all intended for you.

As I grew older the picture became (I hope) a little less self-centred. But it was still a picture of pervasive divine providence. I believed in a personal God who weaves His purposes through all events: in the big public events of history, and in the details of my private life. When I stumbled across accounts of Dunkirk and read how curious decisions by Hitler and fortuitous weather combined to save an army at a critical moment, I presumed it was providence. I made the same presumption when I chanced upon a stranger who provided me with personal advice at the precise moment I needed it.

Such pictures of providence are not rare. A sense of providence is potent, still, in people of strong faith and half-faith. It shapes people's expectations of life more commonly than many care to admit. But is there any conceivable truth in it? Is it not just one of those many beliefs which are generated out of our need for reassurance? It could so easily be just a projection of a psychological need. It is good to believe that God is in control of events, even if we cannot be - *but is it true?*

Biblical faith believes so. The God of Job and the psalmists decrees the weather and orders the oceans. The God of the prophets raises up armies, and mobilizes even unbelievers to fight for Him, working through weal and woe, the author alike of light and darkness (Isaiah 45). Individuals, as well as nations, testify to it. Joseph's brothers may have betrayed him but he is still able to declare it as a creative act of God: *'you intended to do me harm ... but God intended it for good, in order to preserve a numerous people'* (Genesis 50). The God of Jesus is credited with similar power. The Heavenly Father who clothes the flowers of the field and feeds the birds of the air will care for us even more. When evil arises He deftly turned it to greater good: the cross turned to resurrection. In this way Joseph's experience foreshadows the archetypal experience of Jesus himself. They intended to do Jesus harm, and they did: but God was able to bring good out of it.

But how can we believe it?

For me it was a picture of life which crumbled easily. Kaleidescope-like, it was shaken - and it disintegrated. Intellectual enquiry and the raw realities of experience took their toll.

To begin with, scientific world-views seemed to paint quite different pictures. If natural events are interlocked with natural causes what room is left for God? How could any *specific* natural event like good weather at Dunkirk, or Wimbledon, or your wedding (however much you prayed for it), be attributable to God? God might conceivably be author of the whole sequence of cause and effect, but how could He steer any specific moment within it? If all is tightly interlocked, God's intervention would be like trying to alter knitting: the whole thing would unravel. This even seemed true for the causality of events in human history. If there are psychological, sociological, and biological causes for all our human actions, there is no need to invoke God's action to account for them either.

When the science was updated this did not seem to help much either. The world now is not seen so much as a rigid grid of interlocking causes. It is a more malleable mixture of randomness and openness, as well as necessity. This might add the element of risk and chance to God Himself. But most of all it makes it even easier to relegate Him to generalities. God is perhaps the overall author of chance and new possibilities, but still not the one who intends and causes the specific events which emerge from it all. So one way or another scientific portraits of the universe seemed to sit uncomfortably with Biblical pictures of providence. They repaint our portrait of God. God is, at best, only the guiding agent of the process as a whole, not the personal agent of particular events within it.

Then there was the heavy weight of experience. Suffering, as well as science, paints different pictures. This matters all the more now we are so saturated with suffering and evil. Our direct experience of it may be limited, but the miracle of mass communication has exposed it to us massively. There are monumental evils in the world which we cannot evade. This strains the credibility of providence quite as much - more - than scientific theory. In the face of great evils providence seems either desperately limited and ineffective - or callously random. The old questions hit hard at me (and still do, of course). If God could and did arrange events to prevent slaughter and defeat at Dunkirk, why not at Auschwitz, Arnhem, My Lai, New York City? If God can arrange convenient coincidences to guide me in my little world, why not for others when it matters so much more?

The answer most readily to hand again means re-painting our picture of God - as a remote cause rather than a specific agent. Even if God remains the inspiration of the play as a whole, He cannot be the author of every specific sub-plot. God's agency is reduced to a generality. Or else He is reduced to the Spirit alongside His suffering people. God becomes a fellow victim of the chance and necessity of the world He created. He may be able to give spiritual succour to help us endure events, but cannot effectively steer the events themselves. This is an influential picture of God in modern times. Even if God is not remote He is certainly impotent. It has seemed to many the only possible response to suffering. Since we cannot believe in a God who arbitrarily picks and chooses those whom He will help, then we must assume He *cannot* help us.

In this way the kaleidescope shuffled through its new pictures, seeking desperately to make sense of God's action in this wondrous but difficult world; largely failing. I do not think there are many who live and think in this world with faith who have not found themselves on this restless journey between pictures. Sometimes it seems much easier for God to drop out of the picture altogether. For some, of course, He has.

But is this journey always a straight line? Are we bound to move only in one direction: from full-blooded faith in providence, to a generalized, remote, or deist God, to an impotent God, to no God ....? Or is there the possibility of another twist of the kaleidescope?

There is. In fact, there has to be another way of seeing things. Why? Because the new pictures will not do either. Outright atheism certainly will not do: goodness and purpose cry out for explanation just as much as suffering and chaos; the testimony of Christ, and the Spirit within us all, will not lie down and die. An impotent God will not satisfy either. A God who suffers with us but cannot materially affect the course of things faces His own crisis of credibility. The intention may be to rescue such a God from the charge of moral insensitivity: but the effect is to make Him a monster of moral irresponsibility. It would mean God risked creation with no guarantee that He could act effectively within it - and this prompts moral outrage from the creatures at the heart of the experiment. How dare God play so fast and loose with us. Even human parents can steer events to help their children to *some* extent. If they cannot, they are not fit to be parents.

This point must be pressed. If God cannot work effectively within the events of His creative endeavour, He should not have started it in the first place. But He did - because here we are. And since God cannot be a moral monster of such huge irresponsibility, we are made to think again. We must look again at possibilities that God *is* acting effectively within it all, after all, however opaquely, however agonizingly invisible.

It prompts another look at the journey I travelled. Did I yield too easily to the pressures of science - and suffering? Is it really true, for instance, that any account of natural causality so entirely excludes divine causality? Perhaps not. After all, divine causality, by definition, must be a different category altogether. So it might work through other causes, without displacing them, without even being visible. It might work through both 'necessity' and 'randomness' (or whatever follows in future scientific pictures of the world's *modus operandi*). Perhaps it is something like the way my own will works. My mind and intention works through the movement of nerves, muscles, bodily regularities and contingencies - and thereby enables me to do particular things - to lift an arm, make the sign of the cross, hit someone, speak. This operation of mind and will is invisible (you cannot catch it and see it), but it still works effectively through these other structures.

Perhaps God works like this too, analagously, in some such way?

If so, another part of the picture must be re-arranged. I have to consider again the apparent arbitrariness of providence, the weight of undeserved suffering. Is there any way that this too might seem less suffocating, not quite so baffling? In some small way, yes. For if God is (normally) acting *through* other systems of causality, contingencies, necessities, then God is acting jointly. We and the rest of creation are co-workers with God. The world in its very constitution includes a kind of democracy. It involves a kind of shareholding. And that means it is bound to be a long, arduous, painful, weaving of His purposes. Occasionally this joint work comes together swiftly in a luminous, striking way (Dunkirk, perhaps, or some odd moment of personal guidance). More rarely it may even be by-passed in a miracle for some special purpose. But normally it is bound to be invisible, slow, perplexing. That is the inevitable price to be paid for working jointly through this difficult mix of freedom, chance, necessity. It is the way *love* has to work.

Is this still a huge constraint on God's power to act? In a sense it is, because it slows down His ends. But it is not impotence. God is still achieving His ends in and through it *all* - and 'all' includes each specific event. Some of these ends may not be visible until eternity. But the grit of actual daily events has still contributed to them - and that is because of the action of God within them all. Remember again the Biblical stories and archetypes. Remember the pattern of cross and resurrection. Remember the God who works through Judas' freedom to sin, through the political and religious contingencies of the time, through the mental and physical sufferings of His own son. It was all steered towards the unimaginable greater good. Perhaps this is the truth of everything that happens.

In short: providence is impossible to believe as God's special causal mechanism for quickly steering His children out of danger to freedom in His promised land. But it was never meant to be that. It is another way of working altogether. And this is why I found myself returning to the persistent power of the old stories and pictures after all. They play again on my mind and in my soul. Perhaps they never quite left.

Mind you - I return to them, or they to me, chastened. I am no longer so confident that I can expect everything to be clear in meaning, and certainly not as I want it to be. I must concede that we shall not always know what is going on, or like it. All is meant, but only in a wider context of meaning than I can possibly know.

Particular events are still terribly particular and partial. I know they matter greatly, I know they are all essential ingredients in this infinitely complex joint enterprise, but God only knows the final place they occupy.

In one of his novels Morris West writes: *'I found myself drawn with poignant yearning back to the beliefs of my childhood: a personal God to whom not even the fallen bird was unimportant ... Then I knew that I had reasoned Him out of my universe, and that He was forever beyond my appeal'.* There again is the first part of the journey. An almost inevitable spiritual and intellectual journey, in such a world as this. But now I no longer believe it is just nostalgia, nor incredible, to make some sort of return journey. I believe it is possible to move on to a new place more like the place where West began: to a personal God who can and does care even for the fallen sparrow.

2.3 The Clamour for Attention: A Sort of History of the World

Some social commentators like to write history with a single unifying principle through which they interpret everything. Karl Marx, for instance, used the principle of dialectic - especially the dialectic of class struggle. The method has its dangers. In its effort to fit everything into the chosen principle it illuminates some things, but skews others. Nonetheless, the illumination may sometimes be worth the distortion. So I am going to try out a principle myself: *the clamour for attention.*

Natural history could easily be written up this way, metaphorically. Watch (if only on speeded-up film) plants pushing and shoving their way up into the sunlight. They are craving to get noticed by the sunlight. They are desperate for its attention. They will push others aside in the race for it.

Social history is much the same. There is a history of tribes and nations tussling for territory. They do it to survive, but it is also a quest for status. It is a search for power beyond survival, a search to satisfy the need to be noticed, to count, to become a force to be reckoned with. It is true of groups within a society. Suffragettes, Trades Unions, Feminists, Gay Rights and Animal Rights activists - successively they fill the news and set the agenda because they are movements seeking attention. They are people who want and need to be noticed. It may be a means of gaining power. It may be an engine for change. But one way or another the clamour for attention is always woven inextricably within.

Our own personal history is another case in point. We too are attention seekers.

Here, as so often, the child holds up a mirror to the adult. We are usually more subtle about it as adults - but have we really grown out of it? Hardly. We all retain the ache to be noticed and valued. Even those who shrink from public attention still seek to be noticed privately. Perhaps just by one particular person. But always by *someone*. Even those who seem massively secure and self-sufficient seek it. Even (or especially) those who appear to forget themselves and do nothing but pay attention to others need it. We are all sublimating or dissembling some need to be noticed.

Does it matter? Is it good or bad?

It can be bad. It can be a sign of serious sin, a nasty remnant of our evolutionary origins. It can be inseparable from the sort of self-assertion and egoism which thrusts others aside and pushes ourselves forward just to feed our own voracious appetite for self-aggrandisement. Remember the sly serpent of the Creation story who invited humanity to be like God, living for ever, knowing all things, a force to be reckoned with. Humanity did want it - but in reality what we wanted so much was to demean us and bring us low. It damaged our proper relationships with God and with each other. It is a kind of egoism which is pernicious and destructive both to our own soul and to others. Jesus reserved his fiercest attacks for it. Those who paraded their prayers in public places (wanting to get noticed) were in serious spiritual danger.

But it is not all like that. The clamour for attention is not just a sign of sin. It is just as likely to be a sign of insecurity, neglect, oppression. A sign, in today's language, of being marginalized. So when the clamour comes it is often a thermometer of some injustice, a litmus test for life's unfairness. It is often a sign of severe suffering. God Himself, in Christ, cried out for attention: *'My God, My God, why have you forsaken me?'*

The clamour is also just a simple sign of our personhood. It is a sign that we are all constituted as persons by our capacity to relate to others: to love and be loved. We are made by God to reach out and relate because we are made in the image of a Trinitarian God who is essential relatedness. No wonder our hearts are restless until they find some rest in right relationship. No wonder we need attention. No wonder the history of the world is a history of this constant clamour.

But now for the correlate. There is another history pressing upon us just as urgently. There is the history of how God hears this cry. The history of how God *does* pay attention.

It is told in the history of Israel. God attended when His people cried to Him out of slavery. He brought them out of slavery. He gave his commands and covenant to guide them. It is focussed even more sharply in Jesus' life and teaching. Jesus attended when the woman with haemorrhages tugged at his coat. He attended when the roof was broken open above him to let a paralysed man down, interrupting his teaching, crying out to be noticed. Of course he did: *'O that thou shouldst give dust a tongue to cry to thee and then not heare it crying?'* (George Herbert).

The supreme act of attention is the act of incarnation itself. It is the attention and act of love. To become incarnate is the sort of attention a lover pays because it expresses the longing to come inside the life of the beloved. It is God wanting to hear our cry from within, God wanting to know us intimately. Like all lovers God wants to be close enough to see the detail and particularity of our lives, not just the generality. The nature of God's close attention to us is a true lover's attention. The incarnation is the glorious absurdity of paying attention to the very eyelashes, the toes, the tips of the ears, of the beloved. It is the stuff of Valentine's Day messages and (more elegantly expressed!) of John Donne's love sonnets. Moreover, like any true lover, God's attention does not falter when He sees the unlovely in us as well. All this is entailed by the incarnation, that point where both histories - our clamour and God's response - meet miraculously. It is a meeting which the Spirit continues through all time. God the Spirit *keeps* paying us this intimate attention.

But what does God actually do when He attends to us?

The stories tell us. The story of Adam and Eve tells us first that God lets us be. He lets us be free. God does not overwhelm us with His attention. Equally, the stories of promise, covenant, command, and prophecy tell us of His huge commitment to us, His ceaseless concern. They are stories of the Hound of Heaven, always after us, never giving up.

They are also stories of forgiveness and reconciliation. When God meets the people of Israel collectively, and when He meets the individuals who roam the Gospel pages, He so often addresses them with forgiveness. Even those presented to Him to be physically healed may be offered forgiveness.

Why is so much of God's attention paid in acts of forgiveness and reconciliation? It is because our most crying needs often arise from fractured relationships. Even the cry of the physically sick. Even the cry of the socially oppressed. This is not because sickness or oppression is always caused by the victim's own failed relationships, the sufferer's own sin. Emphatically not. Both Bible and common sense tell a much more complex story of cause and effect. Yet forgiveness is still important because suffering is almost always related to someone's sin. There will usually be some fractured relationship involved, indirectly, somehow, somewhere, as cause or consequence, or both.

This means it is not just the egoist's cry for attention which needs forgiveness. The victim's cry may need it too. To be sure, victims may need other forms of attention as well. They may need social empowering, freedom, food, medicine. But forgiveness cannot be ignored. That too may be needed.

There is something important here. Contemporary culture has largely abandoned the abhorrent assumption that all victims are specifically guilty and deserve their fate (though we must always beware a lurking residue of this belief). Thank God it has. But there is an opposite extreme: to sanctify victims, to count them always innocent, immune to the moral mess we *all* inherit. Liberation movements and single issue pressure groups sometimes court this danger. It is dangerous because it blocks off a healing channel which may be badly needed as much for victims as for perpetrators of suffering. That is why God gave authority to the Son of Man to forgive sins anywhere and everywhere - even amongst the sick and suffering.

Of course there is more to our history than the clamour for attention. And there is much more in God's history of paying us attention than the act of forgiveness. But there is no doubt the cry exists. The world is not a silent place. Nor is there any doubt that God hears it and heeds it, in His own way, through Christ and by the Spirit, with healing acts of love and reconciliation.

We too must heed the cry. It is not even in our own interest to block out the noise for we shall only provoke bad behaviour: when people need attention, and do not receive it, they stop at nothing to get noticed. Remember again the child is within us all - and the child cannot be ignored. Thank God that God in Christ has not ignored us.

3. God, Incarnation, Trinity

A suspicion we may be making it all up, and the fear that we have no significance, are both aspects of our finitude. In one way or another we are acutely aware of the impotence and inadequacy of being finite. This is true when we contemplate the universe. But it is also true when we contemplate God. God may well be the solution to the problems of our finitude, but He is part of the problem as well. His power, His perfection and His mystery dog us. God provokes as many questions as He answers. Some of these questions are recurring. We have met them before, and now they ambush us again by a different route.

For instance, if there is a God then our finitude feels more provisional. We begin to dream more dreams. But we still cannot make them happen. Is this simply an irresolvable frustration of our finitude, or is it an intimation of a God who *can* make things happen? Or is that hope, once more, a fantasy we create, itself a dream? And even if God - alone - can fulfil *His* dreams, how does that help *us*?

What is more, if God really is the perfection of our dreams, and beyond our dreams, how can He really be known at all? How can we worship Him? How can He be understood, addressed, spoken of? Must not God be, by definition, beyond definition?

These are the some of the questions raised in this next section, which are 'answered' by the doctrines of incarnation and trinity. This may seem to be an unpromising response of faith. It appears to meet impossible questions with irrelevant answers: technical terms and abstract doctrines. But if we wait to see what these doctrines mean, and if (once more) we see how firmly rooted they are in the concrete reality of Jesus Christ, they become more promising. They also become more personally challenging.

So what do they mean? Incarnation and trinity express the mystery and perfection of God as an incorrigible urge to give Himself away, to act effectively, and to share His life with us in our reality as well as in eternity. In short, to love. As such, love is part of the essential meaning of His divinity and His perfection. But it is also what makes it possible for us to grasp that meaning. His being as self-giving and active love is why we *can* know Him and address Him - as well as why we can and must love Him (and others).

Love is therefore a metaphysical as well as moral key to understanding the mystery of God. Only because of this self-giving action of love can we presume to explore the mystery, as this next section does - as God incarnate and God in trinity, a mystery about love and a mystery revealed by love. In what follows, the book of Job sets the scene for our encounter with this mysterious God. But it is the revelation of God in Christ which gives it the substance. First, this revelation is seen as an expression of the integrity of the divine being. Then it is seen as the expression of relationship at the heart of divine being. Both are aspects of the essential divine *being-as-love.*

3.1 Job, Jesus, and the Worship of Almighty God

It is an old-fashioned religion where God is held in awe and worship offered unequivocally - without question. The strands of Judaeo-Christian religion which sound most out of date to many modern ears are not necessarily its mythological stories but its images of an unapproachable and unquestionable God. We have become accustomed to a cosier belief where God is a friendly sort of chap (still usually a chap!) whose main aim in life is to come close to us and comfort us. Or else God is a shapeless spirit, easily moulded to our desires and created by our questions. I caricature, of course.

Job was ahead of his time. Long before modern fashions, he had the temerity to question the unapproachability of God and His unquestionable ways. The questions of his own tormented existence drove him to it.

Would God yield to this? Should He accommodate Himself to Job? It seems not. Old-fashioned religion duly issued this thundering reply on behalf of God (ch 38): *'I will question you, and you will declare to me. Where were you when I laid the foundations of the earth... who laid its conerstone when the morning stars sang together ... who shut in the sea with doors when it burst out from the womb?'* The irony and imagery is magnificent, even in translation. It is a tour de force to liken the breaking of seas at creation to the flood of waters from the womb at childbirth. And these powerful poetic pictures are all employed to cut Job down to size. Compared to Almighty God a mere mortal cannot hope to understand, let alone question. So Job bows the head (Ch 42): *'I have uttered what I did not understand, things too wonderful for me, which I did not know ... therefore I despise myself, and repent in dust and ashes'.*

Again, good poetry - but is it also good theology? Surely yes - to some extent. If God is God then He will be beyond our reach. There must be a profound difference between God and the rest of reality which brings us to our knees. This is a moral difference. God is holy. It is also a difference in *being*. The difference between God and humanity is not like the difference between adult and child, or even between human and monkey. It is more radical. It is more like the difference between an author and her book, a dreamer and his dream. So of course we cannot understand or question God. We are bound to fall silent and bow the knee.

It is true theology, therefore. But not complete. Although we cannot approach God, does He not choose to approach us? Job did not have the benefit of A.D. We do. We know the transcendent God was also in Christ, that He is also one with humanity; one who *'calls us servants no longer ... but friends'* (John 15). We know Him as personal saviour, as well as holy and incomparable creator. To be both is not self-contradiction. As an author can be truly found within her book, the dreamer in his dream, so the otherness of the creator may also be known in his creation. Transcendence and immanence counterpoint each other. Each intensifies the wonder and surprise of the other. And we worship God for both.

The informal religion of our churches, on the whole, most naturally expresses the immanence and accessibility of God. Thank God it does, in an age when the rumour of any sort of God has become so remote. Our formal religion still more naturally expresses His transcendence, holiness and mystery. Thank God it does, in an age when God is too easily domesticated. But if each could *also* offer the other side of God? That really would be the best of religion and revelation.

3.2 Christmas, Creation, Incarnation: A Story of Divine Integrity

We, poor humans, are disjointed. There may always be some connection between our thoughts (and words) and reality, but there is also some disconnection. We think thoughts, we dream dreams, we express these in words. But what I think or dream or say is not brought about in reality just because I have thought or said it. With our worst thoughts this is no bad thing. With our best, it is a tragedy.

Only in fantasy worlds and stories do thought and word have automatic power to make real. In his stories George MacDonald describes our thought-world concretely, as if it was populated with real living creatures, ready for action. I have some possessive, jealous desire - and immediately a clutching tentacled octopus leaps out to physically grasp those things I want. I have a desire for peace with someone, and a living dove flies out across the gulf between us to carry the message and bring about this reconciliation I have dreamed of ...

It can also happen in the fantasy world of philosophers, even to those who pride themselves on being tough-minded. They too dream of thought passing into reality. The story is told of the philosopher G.E. Moore who had a nightmare where he could not distinguish propositions (thoughts in words) from tables (hard reality). Even when awake, a friend says, Moore could not distinguish love and beauty and truth from the furniture: they seemed to him to have the same kind of reality.

Something important lurks here. Fantasy and philosophy do not just express a longing. They also tell an intuitive truth. In fact our thoughts *do* have some sort of reality, and they *can* have some sort of power. The trouble is, that power is elusive, mysterious, indirect: the limiting fact of the human condition remains.

Sometimes we can think and speak our hearts out yet still produce nothing concrete outside our own minds: like a pianist running over the keys of a piano, without ever producing a real sound. Such limits to our power may be protecting us as much as frustrating us. But either way they exist.

Except at Christmas. Or every time we think of the incarnation. That is when we hear a different story. When we hear of a word which did become flesh; a thought and a purpose which did become a living creature. Like the fantasy, but not a fantasy. This time, it happened.

It has always been so with God.

In ancient Jewish understanding there is no disjunction between God's thinking, words, and reality. God said: *'Let there be light - and there was light!'* (Genesis 1). By God's thought and word not just light but this whole real world came into being.

How? The mechanism is secondary. The point is not in the means, but in the outcome. Whether through big bangs, the expansion of gasses, the dying of stars, or some other means, the inescapable point proclaimed is that the desire of God *took effect*: it happened. Thus Isaiah (55): *'so shall my word be that goes out from my mouth; it shall not return to me empty, but it shall accomplish that which I purpose...'*.

This divine power is at its clearest in the incarnation of Jesus. There it is pre-eminent, and very personal. In Jesus of Nazareth the mind of God becomes an actual living person. God does not just think about humanity, He becomes humanity, not just in abstract generality but in concrete particularity. He does not just imagine overcoming evil in his mind, He does it in reality. He does not just utter words about forgiveness, but expends the effort of actual forgiveness, in flesh and blood. Put another way, Jesus Christ is the complete *integrity* of divine love and divine being. He is the place where God's thought and action are most obviously one. This meaning of incarnation is crucial. It must take precedence over the merely sentimental spiritualizing of the Christmas story, or the theological agonizing about precise causal means (like the virgin birth).

Its meaning also spills over to engulf *us*. The integrity of divine love carries a guarantee for us too. What God did in first century Palestine in the life of one man, He can do throughout all reality. Because of Christ, God's purpose can take effect in us too. Ultimately. Somehow. Again, the mechanism may be opaque, but the meaning is still clear. Because of Christ we too can be in Christ and He in us. As in Adam all die and are disjointed, so in Christ shall all be made alive and whole.

When this is believed and proclaimed it stirs a deep hope. It makes some sense of our dreams. It gives some substance to our fantasies. It resonates with the recognition that our thoughts and longings *are* significant, even though (at present) they have so little causal power. It means that the brokenness of our human condition is not the end of things, but a sign of wholeness to come. It is a wholeness which *has* come, in Christ; and which *will* come to us. It will come when we are ready. Ready to think and will the good, only the good, the dove and not the octopus.

But what about now? What about this meantime when we are not yet ready and whole?

Integrity is still the goal. And although we are denied the absolute power of divine integrity, we are not denied all signs of it. We can be brought alive. We can know eternal life. We can let at least some of our best thoughts pass into reality. By grace, and in some degree. And if we can, we must. God's integrity demands ours, so far as possible. In whatever degree we can we must let our thoughts and words of goodness or of God come alive and take effect in reality. The Gospel of John and the Epistle of James both tell us this: it is not enough to study the words of Scripture, believing that in them we have eternal life; we must come to life in Christ Himself (John 5); our religion must not be a matter of words, but deeds (James 2). Matthew's Jesus tells us the same: '*not everyone who says to me "Lord, Lord" will enter the Kingdom of Heaven, but only one who does the will of my Father in heaven*'(Matthew 7). It is all a matter of bearing fruit. Real fruit.

This integrity is for society as well. It is not just our own individual being that is at stake; society too depends on it for its survival. Society crumbles if people see no connection between rhetoric and reality. Confidence, credibility, authority, all become eroded if people see hypocrisy in high places, if they see a cynical dissociation between word and deed, if they see spin. Only if people perceive some integrity can society be saved and saving. This places great responsibility on leaders and public figures, in politics, the judiciary, commerce, education, the media. They must not leave too big a gap between ideas, words, policies - and reality.

All this is easier said than done. That is the point. *Everything* is so much easier said than done. But what is impossible with men and women is possible with God. That too is the point. It has been done by God in Christ, and so there is a guarantee it can also be done by Him through *us*, in part...even in this meantime and mid-place, this disjointed state in which we find ourselves, stretched and struggling between earth and heaven.

Thank God for the Gospel of His integrity which was born at Christmas, which climaxed at Easter, which touches us all at Pentecost, and which fulfils us finally beyond all history. Do not stop dreaming good dreams. They can take wing and fly across the chasm. They can pass from thought to reality. For they are underwritten by the integrity of divine love.

3.3 Looking at the Sun: Toying with the Trinity

There is an ancient story which tells of the visit of an Emperor to a Rabbi.

I should like to see thy God, said the Emperor.
Impossible, said the Rabbi
But I will see Him! insisted the Emperor.

So the Rabbi led him out into the bright sunshine and pointed upwards. And the Emperor tried to look into the sun, but could not. Its brightness blinded him, and he bowed his head.

Of course we cannot see God. It is both a moral and an intellectual impossibility. How could we look directly into the bright light of utter holiness? How could we even begin to grasp the mystery of supreme being? And if we cannot conceive Him how can we express Him? How can we address Him? Our words and pictures are bound to fail - in one of three ways.

They may reduce God, scale Him down, subject Him to the indignity of being treated just like one of our familiar friends. It is the commonplace prayer of pietists: *'Dear Father, I just want you to know I really love you ... and please, will you help me today?'* - for all the world as if this fickle father does not know what we need and must be flattered and cajoled into action.

Or else our words and pictures will complicate, codify, and abstract God, wrapping Him in the riddles of technical language and impossible concepts. Thus we speak portentously of eternity, aseity, transcendence, and we do so not once but three times over: *'the Father incomprehensible, the Son incomprehensible, the Holy Ghost incomprehensible, and yet not three incomprehensibles but one ....'* The intention is to pay God some sort of metaphysical compliment, but the effect is merely to subject Him to another sort of indignity: that of being addressed like a mathematical theorem (which the theologian is constantly testing to see whether it adds up).

Or else words fail simply by slipping into vacuous generalities, and we do God perhaps the greatest injustice of all: we dissolve Him into a nonentity, a sort of spiritual ether of the universe, everywhere in general, nowhere and nothing in particular. It is the prayer of the New Age: *'O life force, O spirit of all things ....'*

All this - being too naive, or too abstract, or just too vague - is a consequence of trying to look into the sun and failing to capture the fullness of the brightness of God's being. It is inevitable: *'our little systems have their day/they have their day and cease to be/they are but broken lights of thee/and thou O lord art more than they ....'* (Tennyson).

So perhaps there is a lot to be said for not even trying to look directly into God. There is much merit in the merely oblique, allusive, suggestive approach. Perhaps we should presume only to touch the outskirts of His ways through the medium of music, the metaphors of theatre and ceremony, or the unexplained symbols of sacrament: surely safer than words and concepts? Perhaps we should only refer to God as we allude to the presence of an immensely important person at a reception: with discreet glances, veiled references in our conversations, anxious lest we get the title wrong, terrified of presumption. Much Jewish religion was like this: no-one can see God and live; God has no proper name - *'I am who I am'* (Exodus 3). Better, then, to avert our eyes, and our speech. There is much to be said for reticence.

But there is something else to be said as well - if we are Christians. The full metaphysical mystery of God may be beyond our knowing: but has not God also made Himself knowable - in other terms? What else is Jesus Christ but the knowable face of God? This is what we are told in Johanine theology: *'Whoever has seen me has seen the Father ....'*(John 14); *'The word of life was revealed.... What was from the beginning [is] what we have seen with our eyes...touched with our hands'* (1John 1). In the human, historical, tangible event of Jesus Christ God has deliberately filtered His strong light so that we *can* gaze at Him, understand at least a little of Him, even begin to speak about Him. That is what revelation means. (Incidentally, the self-revelation of a 'higher' reality in a 'lower' is not an intrinsically impossible notion: three-dimensional reality can always show something of itself in two-dimensional drawings - it is called perspective!).

This means that we do after all have a licence to speak of God and address Him. God has issued it Himself. He has not stood on his own dignity. He has exposed Himself to our gaze. He has addressed us - and invites us to address Him in return.

Thereby God takes a risk. He risks, precisely, those indignities of being patronized, abstracted, codified, generalized, misunderstood. Just as He risked being physically maltreated and humiliated when He walked amongst us. But God takes the risk willingly - because He *wants* us to know Him, He *wants* us to talk to Him, He *wants* our prayers (and even our theology), as surely as human parents want their children to stutter and scribble their way into as much conversation as they possibly can - even if they do not always say the right things, even if they do not know how to 'show respect'. It is the price to be paid for real relationship. God gave up His dignity for that. He has given Himself away for this.

Dare to look into the sun, then, and this is what we see. A God who gives Himself away. That is the first thing to grasp. Or, rather, it is the condition of grasping anything at all about God. And that in turn means that this self-giving must be something close to the very heart of God. It is something of His essence and very self. God must be *in Himself* a self-giving God. To see God truly will be necessarily to see Him as a movement, a conversation, a dynamic relationship of giving and receiving.

This is the basis of Trinity. Gaze at God in Christ and *ipso facto* we find ourselves seeing a relationship. We see first the constant self-giving between Father and Son: a mutual sharing of purpose, priorities, pleasures, and sorrows: *'I am in the Father and the Father is in me'* (John 14). It is often described as a dance of self-giving love. Then if we look more closely we see the Spirit who is the inspiration of the dance, its music and rhythm, the one who represents each partner to the other, Father to Son and Son to Father: it is as the Spirit hovers between Father and Son at the baptism that the Father is moved to cry *'you are my Son, the beloved'* (Mark 1). All this is the picture of God we see in Jesus Christ: it is, moreover, a picture of the eternal God, for it is a love with which the Father loved the Son *'before the foundation of the world'* (John 17).

In short, the events and experiences of Jesus Christ are a sort of projection into history of God's eternal being of relationship. God projects His own inner life of love into Galilee, Gethsemane, Cross, Resurrection and Pentecost. He does this so that we can see it in human terms; so we can wonder at it; so we can speak of it, and engage with it. He has licensed this. Gaze into this sun and we shall not die but live.

We shall live, that is, if (having gazed) we also allow ourselves to join in. For the same Spirit who draws Father and Son into their dance together wants to make us partners too. The Spirit who helps us pray (Romans 8) also wants to help us live, to pour this love of God into our hearts (Romans 5).

Myself, I prefer to keep myself to myself. I prefer to stand on whatever shreds of dignity and reserve I think I may have. I prefer not to take risks. But how can I refuse? If God gives Himself away to me, how can I refuse to give myself to Him, and others? Indeed, how can I *be* at all? For if this dance of love is the very being of God how can there be any room outside it? For a while He gives us our freedom to play outside: to experiment with self-centred, self-serving little games of life. But that is only so we may learn that these games are not real. *We* are not real when we keep ourselves entirely to ourselves. In the end we must learn to join the dance - or perish. Perhaps we all will learn in the end, perhaps we will not - but learn we must.

Look into the Sun and see all this. See the Trinity, and see what we must let ourselves become. No doubt these words and pictures too have failed to do Him justice. No doubt I have spoken poorly of Him, or worse. But we are allowed to try - and to speak of Him in this way is at least a start, even if it can never be the end.

4. Lent, Easter, Life After Death

The self-giving God of incarnation and trinity meets the questions of our frailty and finitude as nothing else can. But the range and depth of these questions presses us further. Existentially, as well as intellectually, the need to see beyond ourselves, to face suffering, to live through failure, is nagging and remorseless. How can we really hear God's voice from beyond? How can we grasp the hand we believe that He offers? Even if we can, how do we know the voice we hear and the hand we grasp is trustworthy and credible? How can He really be our God and *saviour*? These are not just questions about the possibility for us of knowing and encountering God but about the possibility for God of dealing effectively with us.

It is at this point that faith which is both Christ-centered and transcendent offers its real heart to us. Because God is the God who was in Christ He can help us through this difficult world out of His own experience of living in it: His own experience of suffering, failure, rejection, death. Equally, because God is more than this world there is more to what He can offer than this world affords: God is also the possibility of healing, perfection, resurrection, heaven. It is this Christ-like God who is both within and beyond the world who can save. He has both the moral and metaphysical credibility to do so.

Some of the issues of previous chapters will be needed to make full sense of these divine possibilities. The objective truth and reality of God, the possibilities of providence, incarnation and trinity, all help explicate how He can save. But it will be the actual narrative of cross and resurrection, and the raw experience encompassed there, which will matter most. That is the heart of the Christian response to the frustrated cries of our finitude - especially the cry of sin and suffering. It is not a response which 'answers' all these cries and questions, of course. But it is the place where they are heard, shared, and overcome - by the God who became a crying, questioning sufferer Himself.

So these are the matters which follow. The first reflection is simply a reminder that we must look for help beyond ourselves. Then there is something of the cross, conveyed with help from a brief narrative of someone else's suffering. The questions and answers then move to eternal life: the possibility of heaven, the necessity of resurrection, its meaning here and now. The last reflection tests out these claims of divine salvation against the hard fact of our continued failure.

4.1 Fish, Lent, and the Need to be Amphibious

An ancient Chinese proverb tells us that if we want a definition of wetness we should not ask a fish. The point is clear. If we are wholly immersed in something we are not likely to realize it. It will be so 'natural' to us that we will be quite unable to see our situation clearly. We shall be unable to evaluate it; unable (if necessary) to criticize it.

Someone consumed by the world of work may be wholly dominated by the value of the work-place. Managerial expertise, the manipulation of other people to achieve economic success, power, position, become normal ways of operating. They even drive him (or her) when she gets home. But she may not know it.

An infirm person living alone may be entirely immersed in personal grievances - about the health service, his family, his thoughtless neighbours. His (or her) whole life becomes a grievance. But he may not know it. Fish-like, she cannot feel the wetness of her self-centredness.

Someone very religious may become soaked in self-righteousness, also without knowing it. It is a dangerous state. *'Now that you say "we see", your sin remains'*, said the Jesus of John's Gospel to some of the religious people of his day (John 9). Falling into this state is not hard. A sense of spiritual superiority is a seductive sea to swim in - and the fish simply do not realize it.

A community (religious or otherwise) may find itself with these traits, not just individuals. It is notoriously easy for a community to succumb to managerial values, or self-pity, or self-righteousness, without knowing it. Remember Reinhold Niebuhr's astute observation: groups tend to compromise and mask morality even more than individuals.

Is self-scrutiny the solution? The world seems to advocate it. Perhaps we ought to find the truth by looking within ourselves, if we do it honestly enough - so we are told. It is part of the Enlightenment legacy to believe this. It is also something the Church advocates. Especially at Lent. Rightly, it encourages self-examination.

But how can we be sure we are honest enough? And how do we stop the sort of introspection which merely colludes with self-absorption, smugness, the status quo? Self-scrutiny can be part of the problem, not just a solution. So we need help from beyond. We need to be examined from some vantage point beyond ourselves. And that means we need to be amphibious. We must take the trouble to surface from ourselves. We need to face the shock, and the sunlight, of another environment.

How? Moving physically to a different location or lifestyle can provide a catalyst. But the heart of this experience is spiritual, not physical. It is theological, not psychological. It is God Himself, in Christ, who enters the water with us, and then brings us out. He is the supreme amphibian. Often He does this through the wisdom of others who do not swim in quite the same sea as ourselves. Their voice is precious, because He speaks through them.

So - listen hard. In one way or another listen to His voice from beyond our own world. He comes from beyond, comes within, and leads us out again into a more spacious place. In the end this is invigorating - to discover how much more there is to life than where we are.

4.2 Good Friday

To offer yourself and then be refused, scorned, dismissed: it is a hard thing to endure.

The parent who puts her whole self into a child who becomes indifferent, or worse.

The writer who puts himself into a work which is rejected.

Anyone who extends some hand of help, hospitality, friendship which is dismissed.

It is a cruel experience, one of the worst.

It happens all the time, through all time. People are always being hurt like this. And the fear of being hurt like this is as crippling as the thing itself. Just to imagine we are being laughed at, misunderstood, criticised, rejected, is painful and paralysing. *Toughen up!* (we tell ourselves, or others). If only it was so easy. Does anyone really learn to grow a thick skin? I think the most we can hope is to learn how to live with a thin skin.

Listen for a moment to Christopher Nolan, a physically disabled boy paralysed from birth, able to speak only in grunts and dribbles: listen to his autobiography speaking for us all as he returns home from his first day at school:

Well, Christopher, how does it feel to have all that behind you? (asked his mother).

All his silent pent-up despair burst wide open and poor Christopher cried out loud, forgetting the old adage that big boys don't cry, very sure they must if life hellishly harasses them ... so he cried fullsome tears of thoughtful, shattered, bewildering, bewilderment.

How must I have looked (he thought).

And feebly, his mother and father tried to divine the depth of their sad son's despair (but could not).

Another of this world's scorned, sad, sons, was Jesus of Nazareth. He was despised and rejected. So was God. For God was in Christ. More than that: God, in Christ, was rejected by his own choice. He entered humiliation not just by force of circumstance, or imagination, but deliberately.

Imagine *that.* You and I often do all we can to avoid humiliation: we compromise our conscience a hundred times every day, we exercise a canny survival strategy, all to avoid the hurt of rejection and scorn - even when love and duty demand we face it.

But He entered it voluntarily.

Why?

For our sake.

He did it, declares the Epistle to the Hebrews, to stand with us as a *'merciful and faithful high priest...[who] because he himself was tested by what he suffered...is able to help those who are being tested now.'* (Hebrews 2). He did it so that the almighty and eternal God should know what it is like - not just by abstract omniscience, but concretely as a human individual. He did it to know what it is to be hurt and humiliated; to know what it is to be tempted to avoid hurt by saving his own skin; to know the *effort* it is to absorb rejection instead of hitting back. And out of this knowing, this concrete experience, He is able to *'help those who are being tested now'*: He is able to offer spiritual power to endure hurt when we have to, to fight the temptation to avoid it when duty demands, to forgive rather than hit back. The humanly experienced God is able to help the inexperienced human creature: you and me.

This means God did it (in a sense) for His own sake as well as for ours. God did it for Himself in order to do it for us. He wanted to empower Himself in order to empower us.

One part of this empowerment is God giving Himself the experience of *forgiving* in human terms. He wanted to expend the effort of forgiveness and pay the cost of unconditional love out of the depth of rejection as a human creature. He wanted to cry as one of us, not 'Father I give up on them!', or 'Father to hell with them!', but 'Father forgive them!'. Only then does forgiveness become real. It becomes epistemologically real: we *know* we are forgiven when we are forgiven in human terms. It becomes ontologically real: we *are* only forgiven if God forgives in human terms. Anything else would be a trick of omnipotence.

In this way, with this human cry of forgiveness, God gives himself the capacity to rend the Temple curtain. He opens a new and living way: we are released, we are forgiven. For all time, through all time. The eternal God has taken into himself all He needs for our needs. All the ancient fears we have about our weaknesses and sins can be laid to rest. Hebrews declares this too (Ch.10): '*...we have confidence to enter the sanctuary by the blood of Jesus, by the new and living way he opened for us through the curtain (that is, through his flesh)...[therefore] let us approach with a true heart and full assurance of faith, with our hearts sprinkled clean from an evil conscience...*'.

This is the full measure of his achievement. Out of his own rejection God can stand with us when we feel rejected. He can empower us from His own experience. He can release us from the crippling power of guilt when we have rejected him. He can forgive.

He can do this because He chose this way.

He *chose* to become like Christopher Nolan.

Like a taunted black boy in an English inner city.

Like a bewildered old Englishman on a housing estate whom the children spit upon.

Like a wife faced with the desperate, dawning horror that her husband despises her after years of marriage.

He chose that, for our sake.

My God, what a God. My God, what a Saviour.

4.3 Tadpoles, Ice-cream, and Sex: The Road to Heaven

Is there really life after death?

It is hard to believe, not least because it is difficult to imagine what it could be like. The unthinkable is often unbelievable. The inconceivable is, strictly, meaningless.

But that does not foreclose the question. Take the tadpole for example. Even if we granted tadpoles the power of conceptual thought I do not suppose many would imagine they were destined to life beyond the pond (as frogs). But they are. Being immersed in one mode of existence makes another kind of life hard to imagine: but that does not mean that what we fail to imagine is an illusion. There really are new textures of life awaiting the tadpole. There is the new experience of breathing air. There is the brightness of direct sunlight. In some similar way the bright uplands of heaven may truly await us, however hard to conceive.

But - would we enjoy a different mode of existence? And would we be *ourselves* if we did?

Traditional images do not seem instantly appealing. Are we really supposed to enjoy perpetual praise and heavenly harps? Even feasting might pall after a while. Do we really have to live (as the Bible suggests in Matthew 22) without marriage? And the more positive promise of being 'with Christ' might seem too vacuous to be riveting. True, these are only images and metaphors, attempting to describe the (temporarily) indescribable. But they ought to convey *something* recognizable as desirable. And they must do so to *me* (not to some other wholly different person).

They do - if we are prepared to use them imaginatively. What else is true praise but the self-forgetful appreciation of something (or someone) attractive? What else is great music but the nearest metaphor for a monumentally satisfying paradox - dynamic timelessness; exhilarating repose; restful participation? What else is feasting but an essentially shared and social delight? And what is a state without marriage? Not necessarily an end to special affections but simply an end to exclusive loyalties (necessary in this world to protect us from exploitation, but not in heaven). As for 'being in Christ' - it need not be vacuous. Is it not being in the presence of sheer unbounded love?

If we are still unsure we could ever want these things more than our present desires (and still be ourselves), take heart. A young child may have little conception that anything in life could satisfy him more than a chocolate ice-cream. But his desires will change. There are more things in life than an ice-cream. Sex, for example. So, later still? And through all these changing desires as the child grows up, she is still herself and not another.

Take heart then. Realities may exist beyond our present power of conception. Our desires can change to fulfil us in a new mode of being. It *may* be true.

But is it?

There are intuitions which make us long for it to be true. Who has not contemplated, appalled, the millions of lives lived on earth comprised of little but a short spell of unspeakable suffering. There *must* be some further life for them. Even a long, happy and fulfilled life cries out for more than oblivion - for it was unique, and uniquely valuable. So no life should be left simply to the wasting asset of fading memories. There must be something more. The 'must' here has a peculiar force. Within a humanist world view it only has the force of wishful thinking. But within a theological world view it has logical force which is also a moral logic. If there is a God who can make it true it must be true.

Is there any other evidence?

There are fascinating (but inconclusive) tales from near-death. There are those who have returned from the operating table or the road-side accident to report some glimpse of a beyond. As if they have seen at least the foothills of heaven.

Is there any more solid evidence?

Yes. There is the resurrection of Jesus Christ. Changed, but still himself. There is the Spirit of the risen Christ. To be sure, this is the evidence of faith as well as history and experience. But it still counts: it will not go away.

Is this hope for all of us, or only some?

That is not for me to say. Grace proclaims it is possible for all. And some readings of pauline thinking suggest this is so: *'God was pleased to reconcile to Himself all things, whether on earth or in heaven...'* (Colossians 1); *'As all die in Adam, so all will be made alive in Christ'* (I Corinthians 15). Equally, we have to bear in mind that God is unlikely to bully us into a state we do not desire. We will have to want it. So although there is nothing wrong with ice-creams, sex, money, success, and so on, we shall need to desire other things, other people, a Christ-like life, rather more. If we do not, how can we be saved? But if we do - who knows what eternity will bring?

4.4 Resurrection: The Irreplaceable and Irrepressible

Death is not what it used to be. Our reaction to it has changed. We have festooned it with flowers. Bouquets at road-side shrines, the aching reminder of fatal accidents. Carpets of flowers at places of disaster. The floral tribute to Diana, Princess of Wales. It is not wholly new, but the scale of it has increased prodigiously.

What do the flowers mean? Are they a replacement for fading religious belief? Or are they an expression of belief, a positive allusion to belief in a religiously repressed and inarticulate culture? Pasternak's novel *Doctor Zhivago* tells of flowers at the Doctor's funeral, used to express faith obliquely in a hostile environment. Gloriously, extravagantly, whole bushes of white lilac, cyclamens, cineria, covered the open coffin: *'and in those hours when the silence was unfilled by any religious ceremony, the flowers took the place of the singing and psalms. In unison, like a choir, they unstintingly poured out their fragrance ... they seemed to be accomplishing the ritual...'*. And this particular explanation is offered: the flowers are a sign of new life, the recurring miracle of spring; *'...and so perhaps the mysteries of life and death which so torment us are there to be found in the green of the earth, in the flowering shoots which spring again every year from their beds'*.

How adequate is that explanation? Are the recurring cycles of nature a good symbol for hope beyond death?

In one sense they are insufficient. They fall short of full christian hope. If flowers are about celebrating the cycles of nature then they are only about the survival of life in general, not any particular life. When spring is miraculously sprung, grass emerges, flowers bloom, trees begin their long life - but these are not the same thing which died the previous year: what 'survives' is not the same blade of grass that withered, nor the same tree that was felled. It is a replacement. It may be a member of the same species as its precursor, following a similar genetic programme, but it is still another member which nature provides. It is only like the way our own descendants carry our genes and even our ideas: they remain other people, they are not you and me. This conspicuously fails to express full-blooded christian faith in resurrection. The resurrection of Jesus Christ was not just the replacement of Jesus with a movement of like-minded people who carried forward his ideas: it was Jesus himself - transformed, but still truly himself. Instinctively we know nothing less will do. We want, we need, we hope, that John *himself*, Jennifer *herself*, might live again.

But if (in that sense) flowers are not enough, perhaps they speak in other ways. The image of flowers is powerful and multivalent. It conveys many things at many levels. In particular, it conveys a sense of nature's vitality, its *irrepressibility*. Pasternak's picture expresses this well: they are flowers which *'spring again every year'*. Here flowers speak well of resurrection, because resurrection is also about irrepressibility: the irrepressibility of goodness - and of God. Resurrection is about the fact that you cannot hold goodness down for ever. You cannot hold God down. Not for ever, not even in this life, let alone the next.

Temporarily, of course, the good can be suppressed - as the bullying and threats of the old Soviet system suppressed much public religion in Zhivago's Russia. Faith, hope and goodness can be mocked, marginalized, killed - for a while. But not for ever. Nothing could stop the defiant gesture of love, hope, and belief which the flowers of the funeral represented. This fictional defiance is now vindicated in reality, as the old system collapsed and former faith and freedoms have forced their way up into the sunlight again, as like long-buried shoots of spring bulbs are bound to do.

This is only to be expected. How could it be otherwise? Goodness, after all, is the very life of God, indestructible, rooted in eternity. It is the light which John's Gospel tells us *'shines in the darkness, and the darkness has not overcome it'* (John 1).

Yet we are often pre-occupied with the reverse: the apparent irrepressibility of evil. This is not surprising. We know it from experience, we are saturated in it by the media, and we have been taught to be constantly vigilant about it in the biblical heritage of both testaments: *'sin is lurking at the door* (Genesis 4)...*the devil is like a roaring lion...looking for someone to devour'* (1 Peter 5). Hence the powerful strand of christian teaching which fears the power of evil and chaos, which justifies disciplined codes of personal morality and a strong judiciary to hold it at bay. Quite right. As the last century closed and we recalled its history we are bound to remember rampant and terrifying evil: the horrors of the Somme, Belsen, Bosnia, Rwanda. As the new century begins we again see evil as virulent as ever in new acts of global terrorism, and continued global injustice. And we see it all the time closer to home in the ruthless greed and feeble selfishness which destroys countless ordinary family lives. The same greed and selfishness may also be destroying some of the very patterns of nature which bloomed so eloquently for Dr. Zhivago's funeral. So there is little room for facile optimism, and we ignore sober realism about the power of evil at our peril. Proper attention to evil is critical.

Nonetheless, we cannot forget this other history, and this other prospect. There is also this story of irrepressible good. So is it not possible to be too persuaded by the power of evil? It is a fine line but a real one. Cross to the wrong side, dwell solely in the rhetoric of the power of evil, and we may find we are colluding with cynicism: we find ourselves losing heart rather than genuinely wrestling with realism. But the resurrection message helps us hold the line. It resolutely reminds us that Christianity was not born as a manifesto about evil: it was born out of a manifesto of the power of goodness, the unstoppable life of God.

What follows?

Hope follows. Resurrection gives hope for our unique personal being, in this life and the next: it means there is always the possibility of new life for *you* and *me,* individually. It also gives hope for social justice. The irrepressible goodness of God means that justice too must be irrepressible. This is because God's justice and His goodness are one and the same thing. God's character of goodness is not a shapeless sponge, tolerant of everything, absorbing everything without reaction. It is active goodness. It is love. Therefore it requires justice. Not so much the distributive justice found in the balance in scales and mathematical proportion: rather, the personal justice of right relations, which is the overriding biblical meaning of justice. Whatever hurt is done to others must be put right: it is a requirement of holy love. And because that holy love is irrepressible it *will* be done - if not in this life then the next. Real resurrection makes it possible, necessary, and ultimately unstoppable. This is both comforting and disturbing, depending on where we stand in our relations, with God and others. Either way, it is vital for sanity, persistence, and motivation. In a morally chaotic world we need to know that justice can prevail. Because of resurrection we know it will. It is because of resurrection, as Paul says, that we should be: *'steadfast, immovable, always excelling in the work of the Lord, because you know that in the Lord your labour is not vain'* (I Corinthians 15)

It is vitally important that some of this hope is for now. We do not and must not wait for eternity. What the irrepressible power of God's goodness must and will ultimately achieve in full begins in part here and now. That is the Gospel insistence. Eternal life begins now - and if we have eyes to see we shall see it. Communism has crumbled. Justice was forged (to some extent) in South Africa. Loyalty, love, and sacrifice does abound secretly in a multitude of private lives. We know that this is not the whole story. We know that such signs of hope are partial and often bring new evils in their wake. But we also ought to know that these signs of the good are already at least part of the story.

This is where it becomes particularly clear how resurrection provides the antidote to cynicism - that cynicism with which we collude all too easily. Cynicism comes when we are weary of goodness and cease to believe in it. It grows more likely as our culture gets older, just as older people may become world weary, seeing only the signs of compromise and weakness and sin around and within us all. The resurrection sign of hope, both now and for the future, is the precise christian counterpoint to this. Resurrection reinvigorates goodness by showing its vitality, proving its power to rise out of weakness, compromise, failure, sin. This kind of power is dynamic, surprising. It makes goodness *interesting*. It should, incidentally, make the world's media interested in goodness. They should ferret around after it with as much vigour and relish as they do with evil.

In the end neither the eloquence of flowers nor words can fully express this whole meaning of resurrection. Resurrection as irrepressibility has a transcendent meaning which is only fully expressed in Jesus Christ. He is where both the irreplaceable and irrepressible are found pre-eminently. It is good that flowers, or music, or poetry, or painting, express what they can of the 'mysteries of life and death'. But no natural or human creativities can entirely do justice to the full christian hope within us. We shall also need some reference to Christ Himself as well. He who is the real reason why death is not what it used to be.

4.5 The Other Side of Failure

'Mixed motives .... Every side of our character plays an important part, the base as well as the noble. Which side cheats the other when they stand united behind us in an action? When, later, Mephisto appears and smilingly declares himself the winner, ***he can still be defeated by the manner in which we accept the consequences of our action'.*** (Dag Hammarskjold).

The modern and post-modern world brings a heightened sense of failure. Because it is a complex world which offers so many choices, we are all the more bound to feel we have made wrong ones. Because it is an intrusive world which communicates too much information, we are bound to feel we have not done enough about what we know. Because it is a seductive world forever advertising life-style images of unattainable perfection, we are bound to feel we have failed to measure up. This makes us a disappointed people. Often demoralized. We think we have failed.

Much of this sense of failure needs sifting out. There is real failure, but there is also a false sense of it. There are times when we fail our own deepest beliefs, but other times when we have only failed other people's expectations. Do not lose sight of that distinction. It is a real one in principle, even if it is a hard one to make in practice. The capacity to distinguish what really matters from what social pressure projects onto us is an important gift. It comes to our culture from Judaeo-Christian origins, and with a good deal of help from the enlightenment. The prophets, the ministry of Jesus, and the experience of St. Paul, all demonstrated this capacity. They all made the distinction - and although God alone is able to make the distinction reliably, the fact that it can be made is our salvation. A sense of failure needs it because we need to know there is forgiveness for what really matters, and vindication for what does not. *And there is* - in God, in the end.

But what about the meantime? Here and now there is still this burden. There is the impenetrable mixture, a complex sense of failure generated by a complex world. And we know it is likely to include some real failure, by any measure, even if we do not know how much. So what are we to do with it? What do we let our sense of failure do to us?

Everything depends (as Hammarskjold hints) on how we deal with the consequences.

The consequences of feeling a failure, and how we deal with it, are legion. It can paralyse, depress, drain all colour from life. It is like a bereavement. It can make us savage with ourselves. It can also make us savage with others, if we displace our frustration with ourselves onto them. T.S. Eliot demonstrated that, as Peter Ackroyd suggests in his biography. Struggling beneath the weight of high personal standards and a failed marriage Eliot let fly with *'sudden shafts of ferocity'*. Another consequence is simple denial. We suppress failure, shrug it off, harden our hearts and close our minds. All these are the most familiar ways of dealing with failure - and they all give the devil the last laugh.

Salvation comes another way. It is the exact opposite of depression, displacement, or denial. It comes by lifting our heads high, facing our failure clear-eyed, making amends where possible, then moving on. How?

Here, as so often, God is unavoidable. He both poses the question and offers Himself as an answer. God is the problem and the solution. But either way, we have to reckon properly with Him.

You could say God begins by compounding our sense of failure. His own perfection demands the highest possible standards: *'be perfect, therefore, as your heavenly Father is perfect'*. (Matthew 5). This intensifies the dilemma. If we are just dealing with ourselves, or others, or with a socially created God, we can at least negotiate with the demand. But there is no negotiation with the perfection demanded by a real God, an absolute standard of truth beyond us, as well as within us. This was part of Eliot's problem. It was Eliot the believer who was so hard on himself. This is God the problem.

But, thank God, that demand for perfection is not all that is meant by God. God is not abstract perfection, but the perfection of love and grace. And that includes gift as well as demand.

In fact even the demand itself is also a kind of gift, when it comes from the perfection of God. It can help make us more honest, humble, clear-eyed, setting us free from false striving. Measure ourselves against perfection, after all, and we barely want to measure ourselves at all. Compared to God, we know more clearly who we truly are as finite, fragile 'fallen' creatures, people formed out of the dust and the whole evolutionary process. Reminded of this we see the summons to perfection in a different light. It can only be the kind of perfection which is made out of a multitude of counter instincts from this creaturely origin, some within our control, but many beyond. This is part of the complexity which we must see. It means we are not able to be perfect out of our own resources. Paul's struggle with the law helped him see that. To see this can be a real release, not a condemnation.

But then there is also the direct gift of grace - what God gives us *in* and *for* our finitude and fallenness. The gift is Christ, who is perfect humanity. Christ is given - and in Christ perfect humanity is given to us. In biblical language, we are given a way of being 'incorporated' into this perfect humanity of Christ. It is a gift because it is something which we cannot make happen ourselves. Yet although we cannot achieve it ourselves we are to be made perfect as *ourselves* (not just as his replicas) - and this is possible precisely because his gift of perfect humanity for us has been created from within the same fallen conditions we inhabit. We shall only fully enter this perfect humanity in eternity - but all that is necessary for it to happen is already given, in Christ.

How this incorporation happens, I do not know. How could we know the nature of something whose consummation belongs beyond ordinary causality, space and time? Some analogies may help: we know a little of what it is like to become part of beautiful music we have not made ourselves - or we know a little in love what it is like to become part of another person's much better life and to be transformed by it (without ceasing to be ourselves). But they are only analogies. Incorporation into the gift of Christ remains a mystery. Nonetheless, it is a reality: it is a reality of faith, and it is part of the gift of grace.

Then there is more. There is the grace of forgiveness. That too is given by and in Christ. It is always given, seventy times seven, and with it the release which liberates us for fresh living. Remember (to take just one narrative example) the inspired appendix to John's Gospel where Peter is re-invigorated by the lakeside, post-resurrection, a failure fully re-commissioned. This sort of grace is predicated on knowing the truth about failure (rather than denial and suppression). But it is also a grace which moves us on.

There is also the grace of providence. When we do (genuinely) fail, our failure is underwritten by divine providence. God literally picks up the pieces after us, recombines the elements of the stories that we or others have disrupted. That is the pattern of the patriarchal stories, it is the pattern of Paul's experience and theology, it is the pattern of the cross and resurrection itself: God has the capacity to piece together new good out of the splinters of evil. We do harm...but God intends it for good: in some way all things do work for good. This too helps us move on.

All this is the way of salvation demanded and given by the perfection of God. In the gift of incorporation there is a fulsome recognition that God takes overall responsibility. By incorporation into Christ all our imagined failure and everything beyond our control is just as much within His power to heal as real failure. So we need not worry. Equally, in the gifts of forgiveness and providence there is a way which frees us truthfully from the imprisonment of real failure. The summons of idealism is not suppressed, the need for forgiveness is not denied, but the dynamic of God's action is always to liberate us and move us on.

It is a way of salvation which clearly trumps the devil on his own ground. He can no longer find any corner of our experience to accuse or paralyse us. It is for us only to accept this. As Hammarskjold insists: *Mephisto can still be defeated by the manner in which we accept the consequences of our action.*

5. Spirits, Feelings, Prayers

Feeling, as well as thought, is an essential ingredient in the dialogue of faith and experience. Our felt response to the things and people around us is always revealing .

What do we find within our feelings? The very range, variety and intensity of feeling can make us wonder. Wonder itself is a feeling of significance. It is often taken to be, in itself, a sign of spiritual experience, a sense of the beyondness of things. But how reliable is that interpretation? Here we are bound to ask again about truthfulness, fantasy, revelation - the questions with which we began. For how do we know what is *authentically* 'spiritual' - or distinctively christian - in these feelings we have? To know the answer to this question is going to be particularly important where feelings are a battle-ground between good and evil, capable of all sort of deceits. We shall need to be discriminating before we attribute certain experiences to God. It becomes even more crucial because feeling has become so elevated. In an age which has increasingly replaced Descartes' deification of the reasoning self ('I think therefore I am') with the feeling self ('I feel therefore I am') it is vital to know which feelings to follow. In short, we shall need to follow T.S.Eliot's advice and overcome that inherited 'dissociation of sensibility' which separates thought and feeling. We shall need to re-learn how to 'think our feelings and feel our thoughts'.

Musing further on feelings and moods raises another, related, question. If they are so ambivalent, as well as powerful, should we allow them to determine our view of things at all? Feelings are not all that matters in our quest to see and act truthfully. Is not faith more than feelings? Faith, surely, offers a wider perspective than feelings within which we need to make sense of the world.

Something similar needs to be said about prayer. Just as the meaning of reality is not wholly determined by what we feel at any one moment, so the meaning of prayer is not exhausted by what we can see in any one moment. If any sense is to be made of prayer, especially petitionary prayer, this too will need a wider perspective than our tiny corner of space and time permits us to see. Previous reflections of the possibilities of providence find an echo here.

The deeper resources and wider perspective of faith and theology matter greatly in all these things. We will need them equally to discriminate within our feelings and experiences, to cope with our moods, and to live with unanswered prayer. So this is what the next section offers in response to some of questions of our feelings: a more measured christian response to some of our most immediate feelings and moods - and a brief reflection on the power of prayer.

5.1 Unknown Modes of Being: Wordsworth, Wondering and Pentecost

When William Wordsworth was a boy he escaped once on a summer night by Derwent Water, rowing out across a lake in a small boat. Being a poet, he recollected and recorded his experience later. It is there in *The Prelude,* his long autobiographical poem: *'Out of the dusk ... a huge peak, black and huge ... upreared its head ... towered up between me and the stars ... and, so it seemed, with purpose of its own ... like a living thing, strode after me. With trembling oars I turned, and through the silent water stole my way back ... and for many days my brain worked with a dim and undetermined sense of unknown modes of being...'*

What is this? A small boy's imagination, tinged with a trace of guilt because he had been playing truant? No doubt. But not just that. There had been other experiences when he was an adult: remember, *'a crowd, a host of golden daffodils, ten thousand at a glance, tossing their heads in sprightly dance'.* Nothing fevered or guilt-ridden there, yet he is still seeing them the same way as he saw the mountain peak. In what way? Hills and daffodils alike, he felt them to be more than mere objects in the way, to be surmounted, picked up, used, or dismissed: instead he felt these things to be astonishing, to be wondered at, respected, reverenced. They were things with a life of their own, with their own *'unknown mode of being'.*

The experience is even more profound when we feel this about people. People too can be seen simply as objects in the way, to be walked round in a crowded street. They can be used just instrumentally, for our own purposes, as we use a mechanic to mend a car, a doctor to make us better. But then we do not really see them as people, as persons. Only when we see them with their own life, their own unknown mode of being, only when we wonder at them for their own sake and not just for ours, only then do we see them as a person. It is something we can feel about ourselves. You may be caught with sudden amazement that you are who you are, with your own unique being. Philosophers who have been caught by this state of wonder have been reduced to few words (Wittgenstein). Poets do what they can to express it. Anyone may experience it, feel it.

Such experiences are spiritual. Mystical, if you prefer. The capacity to wonder at the otherness of things or people, to see them not just as an obstacle or tool to be used but as wondrous - that is a spiritual capacity. It is probably unique to humankind. It is also the root of moral sense. For it is precisely when we wonder at others or ourselves that we can begin to treat them properly. It is the bedrock of all real personal relationships, all potential for love, joy, worship: giving worth to the other.

Is this also an intimation and feeling of God? It is at least an intimation of the *way* we should experience God: with wonder at His otherness, His unknown mode of being. It is a reminder we should not use God just to suit our purposes - as much religion does.

Perhaps it is more. Perhaps it is not just an analogy of *how* we should experience God, but also a real intimation *that* God exists. After all, what causes such experiences? What else could create the dynamics of this wonder which plays like summer lightening between us and the objects of our perception? Try as I might I cannot see how the mechanisms of natural evolution alone could create this texture of experience, because it transcends all the normal categories of natural evolution. Instead, there must be within us, and in what we see around us, some other, deeper reality. As Wordsworth has it again, there must be *'a spirit that impels all thinking things, and all objects of thought: a spirit that impels ... a sense sublime of something far more deeply interfused ... dwelling in the light of setting suns and in the mind of man'.* There is. It is the Spirit of God, who brooded on the waters at creation, who indwells all of us, and everything. The experience of wonder is the Spirit of God at work in us.

But is this also specifically the Spirit of Christ and of Pentecost? Is it the same thing as the Spirit which came with wind, tongues of flame and strange languages? Is it the same Spirit who makes us see God as 'Abba', Father? Is this general structure of spiritual experience which makes us wonder and which belongs to all humanity, the same as the specific explosion of spirituality which burst into the world in the christian story?

In one sense, yes. It is certainly the same texture of experience. A rushing mighty wind sounds dramatically different, but it may be less strange than we think. For it is still a way of describing some unknown mode of being, something *other*, blowing where it wills, not where we will. The gift of tongues to speak foreign languages is also dramatic, but again, it may not be so different. For it is still a way of noticing and respecting the otherness of people. Other people are being addressed in their own language rather than being assimilated to the common language of the disciples. Real communication is established, but in a way which respects people's diversity and otherness. The chaos of Babel is reversed - but not by reducing us all to uniformity: instead we are helped to respect and wonder at each other *in* our otherness.

Occasionally this Pentecostal experience appears to be repeated literally. Missionaries in China have found themselves speaking perfect Mandarin. But it is more commonly repeated when tongues become a form of prayer: a communication to God in God's own language. This is characteristic charismatic experience today. When, privately, one strange evening many years ago in Edinburgh, I found myself praying in tongues, I came to understand it this way: the Spirit helping me to reverence God in His mystery and otherness. Perhaps this is something like what Paul is describing in Romans 8: because *'I do not know to pray as I ought...the Spirit intercedes with sighs too deep for words'*.

So these are similarities. Christian experience and the spiritual experiences of all humankind have a shared structure and a common purpose which has to do with respecting, wondering, worshipping what and who is beyond us. It is one reason why true religion should never divide us from the rest of humanity. It should unite us with it.

But there is a difference as well. There is also distinctive christian experience. This is needed. It is needed as a specific saving vitality in a flawed and fallen world where no general spiritual or moral experience happens easily. After all, we have to remember that any spiritual experience has to be fashioned out of a struggle with countervailing instincts. These are instincts of survival, selfishness, power; instincts from our evolutionary origins and from our sin. They are instincts which mean that our first and (in a sense) most 'natural' thought on seeing a tree or a daffodil or a person is not to wonder or reverence - but to exploit, to use it for ourselves. *And against this backdrop the general created structures of human spirituality are not always adequate.*

This is why the Spirit of God has to find new and distinctive forms of entry into our world - to invigorate and redeem the residual spirituality within us. There will be many manifestations of this throughout world religions. The Christian can only testify where she finds it supremely shown. In history this is in the events of Jesus Christ. Subsequently it is when we are drawn existentially into Christ and when our attention is drawn specifically to Christ. This is precisely the distinctive work of the Holy Spirit. It is distinctive in so far as it is Christ centred, and because (as such) it recognizes and helps win this battle of instincts that we all experience - a battle which drove Christ Himself to the Cross and culminated in resurrection. This is what makes the Spirit seem like fire, as well as wind and tongues, for fire is an image of spiritual battle: it has to do with cleansing and repentance, the burning away of rubbish, the stubble of the fields of our fallen lives. As Eliot said, *'We are redeemed by fire from fire'* .

That is something of the full texture of spiritual experience if it is authentically christian. Its substructure of wonder and worship we share with all. But christian experience also has at its heart this Christ-centred and tough-minded realism. Unlike much New Age spirituality it does not simply rely on what feels natural to us. It offers a challenge to it. It reminds us of a battle to be fought within ourselves before we can truly and fully enjoy and reverence people and God, and even just 'the light of setting suns'. It never fails to remind us that God entered this world and our lives in new ways to fight this battle with us and for us. In Christ, and by the Spirit.

5.2 Musing on Moods: Autumn, Harvest, and Creation Theology

Autumn is an apt handmaid to our changing moods. It sends us shafts of sheer loveliness, incomparable colours, liquid light. Then, inextricably, it pierces the moment with signs of decay and decline, the inexorable advance of winter.

Its ambivalence is found in its festivals. It hosts harvest, a celebration of thankfulness for the fruits of the earth and the goodness of God's creation. But even harvest has its shadow-side. Yes - the earth has been good to us: we eat well and enjoy its splendours. But it is not good to all (any more than we have been good to the earth). Nature, like humanity, can be ruthless and unyielding. It is only a creature of God, not God Himself. *'We celebrate the earth, but we cannot be nature-worshippers, except by projecting upon nature a guilded image of our dreams'* (Austin Farrer).

It is the ambiguity of these rhythms and realities of nature which affect the rhythm of our minds and moods. We are so closely bound up with our natural environment that we cannot wholly transcend it. It is much the same with our social environment. Communities transmit mood and morale, as much as nature. A nation, a church, a family, may be powerfully seized with common feeling - which can swing rapidly, and sometimes inexplicably. Again, an individual within it feels hard put to resist or transcend it.

But should we? Should we even try to rise above our moods?

In one sense there is an arrogance in trying too hard. Why should our personal feelings be exempt from the ambiguities of our natural and social context, of which we are a part? But in another sense we are right to try. If God is beyond nature, as well as within it, and if He is more than a merely social construction, then the yearning for some vantage point beyond the flux of our feelings is not fantasy. It is spiritual reality. By whatever name it passes, it (He) is a vital foothold beyond our fickle feelings. Poets point to it tentatively, allusively: *'a still point in the turning world'*. (Eliot) Paul identified it more robustly in Romans 8. It is the unswerving love of God, shown in Christ, from which nothing can separate us: *'neither death nor life…nor things present, nor things to come…nor anything in all creation'*.

Such love of God in Christ will not take us out of the flux of an uncertain, turning world, nor the moods it imprints on our minds. As long as seed-time and harvest remain we shall remain moody people. But this love will take us *through* the world with a vision from a vantage point beyond it all. It shows us the end from the beginning. It tells us that autumn's ambivalence is not the final word. It assures us that loveliness and goodness will eventually be released from its accompanying decay. It may not banish our moods, but it will help us not to be wholly at their mercy.

5.3 Freedom, the Future, and the Power of Prayer

An exchange of views between a former Archbishop and a Jewish Scholar is instructive. They were debating the power of petitionary prayer.

The Archbishop believed that prayer can sometimes change the future. This is possible because the future is unfixed and unknown, even to God - and it coheres with much modern physics, the Archbishop thought. It means that God waits on our prayers before deciding how to help us shape the future. It is a world of freedom, for ourselves and for God - but the price of this freedom is radical uncertainty about the future, even for God.

The Jewish Scholar was not impressed. If God does not know the future then how can we believe God's promises? The God of the Bible consistently offers promises (not least the promise of a Messiah). These cannot be just pious hopes and divine bluffs. They must be based on God's control of the future. So God cannot be imprisoned in time like us, and this is a world where we and our prayers have little freedom to change ultimate things, which belong to God alone.

Who is right?

As so often, I suspect a false alternative.

Try another picture, combining the best of both world-views. God does indeed know (and inhabit) our future. But precisely because God inhabits our future He also knows the prayers and actions we are (freely) going to offer. So God can, and does, take them into account in the way He helps shape reality in the future. In this way there is both human freedom and a sure outcome. There is a coalition of human contingency and a final cause, all steered by the hand of God.

What would this mean? How would we experience it?

Meaning and experience is determined by context - and the context of what we are trying to envisage is a world of huge complexity. It is a web of almost infinite intricacy where a multitude of natural causes, human freedoms, sin, and divine action interrelate. This means the way in which God takes account of prayers within the web will not always be evident. It means we may not always recognize the answers we hope for. That is the inevitable outcome of a coalition of causes in a complex world. But it still allows that prayer is part of the coalition, a member of God's chosen government: it is 'answered'.

The Archbishop and the Jewish Scholar (and many a modern philosopher of time) will have objections to this picture as well. But I am not lightly going to abandon it. It marries so much of Scripture and experience. It teaches that we are both free and constrained. It teaches both that prayer is answered and that its answers are often opaque, or delayed. *'Ask, and it will be given to you...'* (Matthew 7); yet also: *'not what I want but what you want'* (Matthew 26). It assures us that God can keep His promises, grounded in the great *I AM* which stands beyond time and tense to ensure He can; but it also refers some promises forward to fulfilments beyond our present imagining.

So what? So we should not lose heart when we pray. We should continue to pour our longings into the web of this world's winding course. They *will* be woven in.

6. Morality, Merryness, Pleasure

Moral feeling, like spiritual feeling, invites us down some interesting pathways, raising more leading questions. The fact that our contemporary culture has lost much of its common moral framework is itself an urgent question. It sets us on a quest to find some new way of living together. The very fact that this quest seems urgent is also interesting. It suggests we have not lost the intensity of the moral quest itself. That quest, I believe, is alive and well - and bound to return us in the end to its ultimate source: to God. Morality, as we shall see, is eloquent with transcendence.

But of course, to associate morality closely with God raises its own questions. It sharpens an old conundrum. What is morality actually *for*? Is it for our fulfilment? For our happiness? But if so, why does it sometimes seem to take us on such a hard journey? Why does it sometimes require so much self-denial? Why are we offered the tantalizing gift of so many good pleasures in life, only to be told (or to discover) we cannot always have them? This paradox is harder to bear when these calls to sacrifice are specifically construed as the will of a God who is supposed to be love.

The response will include another set of doctrines: creation, fall, redemption, judgement and repentance, grace and recreation. But again, these are not just abstractions. They do not just codify our experience. They match the hard journey of our experience with the journey God has taken Himself, with us and for us. They speak of the God who has given us all things richly to enjoy - but who has also shown us Himself *how* to enjoy them truly: how to find a true fulfilment in a difficult world where little of real worth comes without some sort of struggle.

This last section takes moral experience very seriously. But only as part of a wider experience, and understanding, of God. A God *'from whom, though whom and to whom are all things'* (Romans 11).

6.1 Moving on from Moral Confusion

Moral confusion is easy to pinpoint. Different things matter (morally) to different people. For some the sanctity of marriage and stable family life matters as the central bulwark of all healthy social order and decency - an order which is threatened by adultery, homosexual practice, 'easy' divorce. For others the enlightenment and romantic ideals of freedom and self-fulfilment matter much more: sanctity is given instead to individual rights of self-expression, whatever sexual or social form they take. There is also divergence about definitions of life and hierarchies of value. We do not all agree about the relative moral significance of the human foetus, the comatose, the dolphin. There is an emerging conflict about bio-technology and the moral nature of genetic manipulation.

In these and other matters we find it hard to agree, and words pour out from social commentators in the endeavour to describe the situation. We are privatized, pluralist, post-modern, and so on. We have consistently failed (especially since the enlightenment) to find a common basis for morality in either reason or religion, so we simply live in the fragments of the past and the random selections of the present. There have been periods of pluralism before, but rarely so acutely documented and painfully self-aware.

Faced with the impossibility of moral consensus, yet still needing to construct some sort of shared social order, what have we done? One analysis has become particularly persuasive over recent decades. It is Alasdair MacIntyre's - and it goes like this. We have redefined the 'moral'. We have transmuted morality from ends to means, and from virtuous character to efficient performance. We have taken refuge in pragmatic, managerial values. What binds us together are values of efficiency, accountability, the capacity to succeed at a given task. The moral value of the task itself (being a soft-ware designer, advertiser, police officer, priest, arms manufacturer) may be contentious and left to private opinion. But what we can agree about is performing it effectively. That becomes the 'moral' issue. The outcome? A society in which we can agree what it means to be a good manager but not what it means to be a good human being. It is a situation which would have greatly puzzled both Aristotle and Jane Austen.

I see much truth in the analysis. But it is already becoming dated, and it is bound to be. That is because such a society is unsustainable. It will fly apart if it has nothing but managerial values to hold it together. The symptom of this already exists in the formation of sub-groups, sects, single-issue movements, as MacIntyre himself recognizes. These withdraw from wider society to offer more red meat in their morality and a more cohesive community to sustain it. But also, there is the new quest for an overall communitarianism – a sign that we find it hard to settle either in splintered sectarianism or in a wider social order which is morally feeble.

One reason is the residual energy of the (truly) moral impulse. By this I mean the impulse that some things really do matter; that the *weight* of mattering can only be described in moral terms of right and wrong (not just expediency and inexpediency, nor just efficiency and inefficiency); and that the *nature* of the mattering must have something universal about it (whatever the disagreement about particular cases). This sense will not easily lie down and die. It will not easily withdraw into self-serving sects or wither into pure pragmatism.

The persistence of the impulse demonstrates itself in the way it finds new channels for its energy when otherwise diverted. We see this in the matter of efficiency - specifically in the weight of indignation and anger brought against those who are negligent about efficiency. Whence the fury in the quest for accountability after accidents and public disasters? Whence the passion behind the burgeoning industry of litigation in matters of damages and compensation? Is it just an expression of grief or greed? I do not think so. It has a moral intensity as well, as if the moral energy of individuals is so frustrated by confusion in most areas of life that it fastens all the more vigorously on the one area where it can have agreed public expression: efficiency. We must be efficient, expert, accountable. We *must* not be negligent. The 'must' here has assumed the same sort of intensity as when we used to say we must not betray or commit adultery. Perhaps it should not, but the fact it has is significant. It bears witness to the irrepressibility of the moral impulse.

But what is this impulse and energy? If it is so easily displaced (e.g. onto efficiency) is it just formless energy? No - because it does not attach itself indiscriminately to anything and everything. Even efficiency is by no means worthless. Also, the very fact we have some sense of *dis*placement implies there is a more proper place for it, somewhere. Moreover, there is at least a common direction within it. The impulse is always driving us out from beyond ourselves towards others, or at least towards a task. What is right always includes some element of self-transcendence, even if it also includes self-fulfilment. What is wrong always involves some element of self-preoccupation at the expense of others.

We need to account for this basic moral impulse. What is its ultimate origin? Is it really just a sublimated survival (or pleasure) instinct, as Durkheim, Freud, Dawkins would have it? Is it only a subtle way in which the individual, gene, or social group secures its own survival - generating just a notion of (moral) selflessness in order to produce the co-operation necessary to survival? Is it, in other words, just a deception: expediency and self-gratification in disguise?

It could be. But if so, why can we see through the process and declare it to be a deception? Its subtlety has not worked. This makes the deception story conceptually implausible.

It is even less plausible experientially. Think again about the feel and texture of the impulse. What is it like to feel the intense repulsion that something is really wrong? What is it like to see a child maliciously hurt? It is to recoil with a weight of feeling which is unique. It demands its own categories, its own language. Expediency or survival simply will not do. Likewise the experience of the right and the good: to see love in action summons us with an intensity akin to the attraction of great beauty. This too demands its own language. It cannot be reduced to survival or pleasure.

Therein lies the best hint of its origin. The commanding push and pull of the moral impulse is like the command of someone's will. It is like meeting the impulse of a powerful personality, experiencing the claim of their loves or hates as our own. So perhaps it *is* just that. Perhaps it comes from something like a person. Perhaps it does not just come as an impulse from evolution (though it may come *through* evolution), but an impulse of the will of a personal God. Perhaps it is that of which the New Testament speaks: the universal law, *'the law written on the heart of Gentiles ... the light which enlightens everyone'* (Romans 2; John 1).

Culture, circumstance, and sin have filtered it, of course. They both transmit and distort it. Sometimes they splinter it into a myriad conflicting fragments. That is the moral confusion we experience. But still this basic form of the *moral* impulse is discernible. It remains, precisely, a moral impulse. It is pervasive and powerful, refusing redefinition and reduction alike. It is not enough to unite us in a common morality about particulars. But it is enough to keep us searching for it. It constantly sends us back (and forwards) to rediscover our common moral roots. It reminds us that we can all still recognize the cry of a child and the love of a saint.

So do not be paralysed by plurality in the moral world. Do not retreat either to cynicism or to the shelter of a sect. Instead, be impressed by the persistence of moral energy in us all. Be moved by its most basic impulse, which takes us beyond ourselves and regards others, which ultimately takes us to God Himself. As we are advised (Philippians 4): *'Whatever is true, whatever is honourable, whatever is just, whatever is pure...if there is any excellence and if there is anything worthy of praise, think about these things'.* Then, having filled yourself with these things, let your heart run back up through them to their origin and ultimate source - to God.

6.2 Eating, Drinking and Being Merry: In Praise of Pleasure

Money, goods, food and drink: consumer pleasures in the material things of life. Some of us in this cruelly inequitable world can enjoy them. But are we allowed to? The liberal conscience finds them haunted by a ghost of doubt. So does the Christian. Is it because of the injustice of inequality? Or is there something in the very notion of pleasure which contaminates itself? It seems subject to the law of diminishing returns. Is this a warning? Where do material pleasures come from?

C.S. Lewis's imaginary devil in *The Screwtape Letters* has no doubt. Pleasure comes from God. All kinds of pleasure. *'Never forget that when we are dealing with any pleasure in its healthy, normal, satisfying form, we are, in a sense, on the enemy's* (i.e. God's) *ground. It is his invention, not ours ... All we can do is to encourage the humans to take their pleasures ... in ways or in degrees, which he has forbidden ... He* (God) *is just a hedonist at heart ... at his right hand are pleasures for evermore. There are pleasurable things for humans to do all the day long without his minding in the least: sleeping, washing, eating, drinking, making love, playing, praying, working. Everything has to be twisted before it's any use to us.'*

Lewis's devil is right. He knows his biblical doctrine of creation. He knows *'God saw everything he had made and indeed it was very good'* (Genesis 1). He knows that *'everything created by God is good, and nothing is to be rejected ... for God richly provides us with everything for our enjoyment.'* (1 Timothy 4 & 6). And he knows this really does mean all things, spiritual and material. It means all the things that Jesus enjoyed - Jesus the 'wine-bibber' who feasted with friends and told stories about the good things of life. What J.S. Mill grudgingly calls the lower pleasures that a pig would enjoy (like eating) are to be enjoyed as God's gift just as much as the higher pleasures that Socrates would enjoy (like poetry).

This is the heart of the Christian doctrine of creation. It has had to fight its corner against various world-denying philosophies, from Manicheism, to Monasticism, Puritanism, and even the liberal conscience. But it has never been written off. Nor should it be.

So whence that ghost of doubt? And why is it a battle to maintain the doctrine?

Lewis's devil puts his finger on this too. He does not just know his doctrine of creation, he knows about the fall. He knows these pleasures can easily be twisted. We know this too. That is why we are haunted, even in our pleasures. We know how easily we can be encouraged to take our pleasures in the wrong way. This is the story of the garden, where the foundational pleasure of freedom is taken in the wrong way - as Adam and Eve both choose to eat a forbidden fruit. It leads inexorably to the spoiling of the pleasure. It is the story of us all, not just our ancestors. What happens to Adam and Eve happens to us. Pleasures which could be fulfilling become destructive.

Again, this is about all kinds of pleasure, spiritual and material. The pleasure of prayer may be taken in the wrong way. How easily it becomes self-righteousness. Material pleasures are even more obviously corruptible. The pleasures of drink can become the destructive demon of dependence. The pleasure of prosperity and the love of beautiful things can become the snare and delusion of possessiveness. It is easy to become trapped in the fear of losing what we think we possess. It is as we were warned: *'...if riches increase, do not set your heart on them ....do not store up for yourselves treasures on earth, where moth and rust consume and where thieves break in to steal.'* (Psalm 62, Matthew 6). The trap is more deadly still when we begin to experience that law of diminishing returns: an ever increasing craving for an ever decreasing return of pleasure. It is as if the pleasures of food, drink, possessions, like power and prestige, are addictive. So much will no longer satisfy, only so much more. In other words, what makes them good can also make them dangerous. There is a drug-like demon lurking in their shadow. Taken in the wrong way, its poison seeps out.

This easy corruption of things which are good in themselves is at the heart of the christian understanding of evil. It means there is no such thing as evil in itself: it is all a twisting and corrupting of some good creation of God. The devil himself is a fallen angel. Pleasure itself remains God's good gift, but pleasure taken in the wrong way remains the root of all evil. And that is why pleasure is both holy and haunted.

How does it happen? Precisely by 'storing treasures up' *for ourselves.* The trap is sprung when we grab and hold pleasures for ourselves, rather than receiving them gratefully to share with others. Like sexual pleasure. The snare of sexual pleasure begins if I seize it as a gratification for me, rather than receive it gratefully as a shared commitment for us. It is the same snare for society: the snare begins when we seize the world's resources for ourselves, rather than being grateful stewards of them for the world. Pleasures must be kept moving between people to remain true pleasures. With active love and distributive justice nothing need go wrong. But without them, everything will go wrong.

Put another way, the snare lies in taking pleasure as an end in itself and living for it in itself. The solution lies in taking it as part of something else - as the gift of a giver, the currency of a relationship. We can be like children who run off with the sweets to consume them alone, left with nothing but the fading taste. Or we can enjoy them as the gift of love from our parents, sharing them in their company and tasting the love as much as the sweets themselves. We can be the prodigal who runs off with our share of the goods, left with nothing but regrets amongst the swine. Or we can return to enjoy the fatted calf as part of our Father's love.

Such is the inevitable ambivalence of pleasure. It is another price we pay for the foundational gift of our freedom.

So what shall we do? How shall we enjoy ourselves better? How shall we enjoy ourselves with love and justice? What other doctrines avail us here?

There is judgement. A ruthless honesty about ourselves will be necessary. Because we are good at deceiving ourselves, this will not be easy. But sooner or later truth must dawn. We must see the truth about ourselves before anything else is possible. And there is little doubt what that truth is. The truth of our situation as a whole is a world of unfettered, galloping consumption by the privileged, driven precisely by an ever-increasing craving. It is a frenetic activity which has found no real way to let its vigour benefit the rest of the world. It leaves millions in shameful deprivation. It does not even make the privileged happy: we are strained and unsatisfied people. That is the whole point: the pleasure corrupts itself when taken in the wrong way. But can we see this? We must. That is judgement.

Then there is repentance. There is the need to turn round, individually and corporately, to exercise restraint, to stop taking pleasures in the wrong way and share them in the right way. Self-denial is sometimes necessary for this. Not because self-denial is intrinsically virtuous but because a corrupted and fallen world sometimes requires it to lever us out of the trap which has snared us. Jesus' call to deny ourselves and take up our cross is not an end in itself, but it may be a necessary movement *within* the journey of redemption.

What form must this turning take? The complexity of the global order sometimes makes this hard to know. But whatever the difficulties, the issue must be on the political agenda in some way. World debt and fair trade must surely be tackled as part of that agenda. The issue must be on our personal agenda as well.

We are not relieved of personal repentance just because the issues are global. Even old rules like tithing and fasting could be dusted down and pressed into service. Such rules will not get us to heaven. They do not have any intrinsic merit, and they carry their own dangers. Nonetheless, they are still a useful lever to rescue us from the traps of possessiveness which enslave us.

But there is grace too. Grace is God's initiative in all this. It is His help - the mainspring both of judgement and repentance, and also their completion in redemption. Grace is God offering Himself in Christ as the truth, the way, and the life: His own experience and pattern of being a fulfilled human. Grace is God's offer to do all that has to be done with us and for us: *'for God all things are possible'*, we are told in Mark 10 even as the rich young ruler sadly went away. Grace can also give back. It may require judgement, repentance, denial - but it can also give back a hundredfold (Matthew 19), *'able to accomplish abundantly far more than all we an ask or imagine'* (Ephesians 3). Grace, therefore, is the eternal return. It is the point where the end is in the beginning and the beginning in the end. In the beginning God saw all that He had made and saw that it is good. At the end all things will be added unto us, for in God's presence there is *'fullness of joy...pleasures for evermore'* (Psalm 16).

So pleasure is very like grace. It is God's first and last word, whatever else is required between. It is part of both creation and redemption. Thanks be to God, who really is a hedonist in His eternal heart.

EPILOGUE

The Portrait Painter

The artist knocked and entered the room, proudly. This was the climax of his career, the finest opportunity. He was going to paint a portrait of God. He set up the canvas, and began to paint.

But the Divine Subject would not sit still. God was everywhere, and nowhere, all at once. It was irritating. It was not appropriate to tell such a celebrity to behave. But the artist needed to assert his authority in some way. So he channelled his frustration into the strokes of his brush. The painter himself began to move quickly. He snatched at his strokes and wove them fiercely together, as if to pin down his elusive subject by the lines he drew and the layers of paint on the canvas.

He stepped back to survey the result.

'Well?' asked the Presence.

The painter barely heard. He was intent on his picture. At first it appeared merely a confusion. Then, as reality met perception, it resolved into a pattern. It was indeed a face. But it was his own. A self-portrait. And he did not like it. It was huge and gaping, deathly. It swallowed everything into itself. The painter felt sick as he looked at it. He was dizzy and faint. He cried for help.

When the painter came to himself he was limp and drained. He looked again, nervously, towards the canvas. It was still there.

But the Divine Subject was not in His proper place. God was still moving. God was (mostly) in front of the canvas, painting over it Himself. The artist watched. God wielded the brush with some dexterity. He was weaving harsh lines into the curve of an open smile. He was planting the angry marks into the depths of eyes to make them wise, wondering, compassionate. The face was smaller, but part of something bigger. There was now a hint of a landscape beyond, other figures within it.

Then for a moment the Divine Presence was still. God too seemed limp, drained. Utterly. But He spoke. *'Well?'* - God asked again.

The artist gazed at the picture. *'I don't understand'*, he said. *'Is it you - or me?'*

But God was off on His travels again. His laughter poured round every crevice of time and space in the room, and out beyond, through windows and doors. *'Why'* came the Voice (still laughing) *'why do you always ask the wrong questions?'*

Then the God said: *'I will ask the questions now'*.

'Do you like it?'

'Do you want it?'

The artist had no doubt. *'I do'*, he said. *'I do...'*

The Voice responded instantly, simultaneously. *'Then let us make more in our own image!'*

The Voice echoed. We hear its echo in many times and many places and many people. And we know that echoes do not come from nowhere.

Index of Names